To Philip
My faithful wingman and num

First published August 2017
Revised and extended edition June 2018

Chapter One

Sitting in the hospital waiting room in a blur of emotion, I find myself suddenly aware of everything around me. The speckled finish on the walls, the NHS blue vinyl flooring, the lines of fixed blue chairs, the bright signs telling me to wash my hands. As my eyes wander around they catch those of the receptionist, we make contact for the briefest of moments and then look away quickly. This was not a moment I wanted to be in, I was used to the long parade of hospital visits as my father's deteriorating health meant we were constantly being bounced from one consultant to the next in an attempt to find the cause. I was used to being called through and told that they could find nothing wrong, so they were referring us somewhere else. Today was different, we were ushered into a room while the doctor gently broke the news that my father had advanced lung cancer. There is that single moment when you hear devastating news, it's like having a stomach punch. You feel the pain, the emotional sweep that runs through your whole body and the numb sense of disbelief.

In the dim light the doctor proceeded to show the scan results and point out the various clumps of cancer which had worked their way through the lung while I tried to absorb the information, my father just sat quietly with his head dropped to his chest, completely lost in his own thoughts. There were a thousand questions, but the only one that seemed of any interest was the simply 'how long have we got?'. While there were the usual caveats the basic gist was six to nine months.

It was suggested that we go and get a drink, have a chat and then come back so they could drain the excess fluid which was building up in my father's lung. I wheeled my father to the only free table in the little Costa coffee, surrounded by nurses and chatty family groups, while we sat with our coffee in virtual silence. Usually my father was the life and soul, full of stories and comedy one liners, but today seemed devoid of anything cheery. All he could say was 'I didn't think this would happen to me'. And I can understand why, he was the strongest man I had ever met, with inner sinew strength and an iron will to match. I had not known my father be beaten by anything.

Back in the waiting area I could feel the emotion beginning to bubble, I had never considered life without my parents. They were such an integral part of family life, it was such a stark wake up call to realise that was soon to come to an end. With eyes full of tears, I called my sister who was taking her usual summer long vacation in Cornwall.

"Hi Cazzy, what's a happening, is everything alright?" came the bright voice on the end of the phone
"It's not good news"
"Oh god, what is it?"
"He's got lung cancer and it's quite advanced"

There was a long pause and I could hear the sharp intake of breath, then came the reply with a voice trembling with emotion

"How is he taking it?"

"Not too well, he can't believe it"

She started to cry which made me well up, so through the sobs we agreed I would call again that evening and we could talk more then.

I drove father home in virtual silence, struggling to get him out of the car after his treatment, back into the house and onto his favourite chair. He told Mum who simply kept saying 'No, you've not got it, I don't believe it. Not you'. After they had both settled with drinks and a small evening meal I left them and made my way home.

This was turning into quite a year. I had always considered myself an extremely blessed individual – I was happily married with three gorgeous grown girls. I loved my work in a large corporate and we both earned a decent amount of money, so life always had those lovely little perks ; lovely holidays, nice meals out and the ability to buy things when we needed them. It had been that way for as long as I could remember. Yet this year was the reality check, things can change in a moment and when you least expect them to. Only weeks before my entire team at work was called into an impromptu meeting. As I entered the large conference room at head office there was a rising sense of alarm at the amount of people who had been invited. And when I say invitation, it was actually more like a summons. People nodded, smiled and passed a few pleasantries while we waited for whatever was coming next. Obviously there had been a huge amount of conjecture about the nature of the meeting; some speculated that we were being merged with another department and a few doom-mongers thought the department was going to be closed down. Most dismissed this as twaddle as we had been brought together as a bright new venture only eighteen months earlier with a huge amount of investment and we had already begun to shake the market and make some good returns.

After a good fifteen-minute delay the department head and his direct superior entered the room and everyone stopped what they were doing. Without saying a single word, we all knew this was not going to be good news, as we watched the man who had led and inspired us all for more than a year stand there with red eyes holding a piece of paper which was visibly shaking in his hands. He thanked us all for coming and explained that he had to read the statement word for word, as it was written. We sat there in that windowless conference room as one department after another heard they were being made redundant. This was then followed by a sickly insincere address by his superior assuring us that our wellbeing was of upmost importance to her and she would do all she could to make sure that this process would be as painless as possible. She had already earned the reputation as a self-serving hatchet lady, who had a history of closing down rather than building up; her address was greeted with a fair degree of eye rolling.

On the train back from London I sat by the window, breathing in the horrible industrial smell of the hot air conditioning and the lingering odour of cooked food. In the distance there was the sound of different commuters taking calls on their phones, some busy with gossip and others confirming business meetings. As I stared out of the window I felt both a sense of sadness yet there was something else, a peace, as though this was meant to happen, it was part of some bigger plan. The strange thing about being part of a corporate is the sense of being locked in. It is like taking holy orders, the job takes over your life and you have to be available whenever you are needed. If that report needs doing, then you work on it, even if it takes you all weekend. It is very rare that anyone contemplates leaving and there is a sense of wonderment when someone does. Why would you want to leave a company with a great pension scheme? And health benefits? And a company car? They must be mad. Yet suddenly there was a sense of freedom, a glimmer that there was a life out there that I had not experienced, and I now had the opportunity to do it.

The garden leave began, with six months to hand over any accounts and important files, but generally to give you a chance to start looking for another job. It was during this period I found myself sat in a consultants' office finding out that I was soon to lose my father. It seemed that I had been given a glorious opportunity to make the most of having him while I still could. The last few years had been very full on as I worked my way up the corporate ladder, and the time spent with my parents had become less and less. I decided that I would spend the last few months of my father's life looking after him and think about my future when the time came.

Thankfully my sister was as committed to supporting as I was, so between us we took on the responsibility of caring for our parents. It actually became more of a full time job than I could ever have visualised; endless medical procedures, daily district nurse visits, dietary requirements, the list goes on and on. My mother, already in her eighties, struggled with mobility and had relied heavily on my father to do everything, so now the responsibility rested firmly on mine and my sister's shoulders. It was endlessly repetitive and emotionally draining. Both parents looked with eager expectation for you to lift their spirits and bring a bit of sunshine to their day. One of the strategies I deployed was to suggest we all sit and watch one of my father's favourite films together and so we did. The African Queen with Humphrey Bogart; The Quiet Man with John Wayne and dad's personal favourite White Heat starring James Cagney. It was on one such afternoon that my father looked at me and said "I remember you always wanted a horse as a youngster. Do you still like them?"

"I do dad, very much. I'd have one tomorrow"

"I thought so. Now go into my planner and find the documentary on Seabiscuit"

We sat and watched this fascinating story together and occasionally I would glance over and catch him watching me. I knew exactly what he was doing, drinking in the moments while he still could. The final climax of the programme came with a thrilling race between Seabiscuit and the current darling of the racing world War Admiral. We had been told that race strategy for Seabiscuit had been determined by Charles S Howard, an un-personable man who had a rare talent for producing winning horses. He had found Seabiscuit when he was a failed track racer and bought him at a bargain price. When asked how he knew that the horse was a winner, Howard said the horse had looked him squarely in the eye with an unwavering sense of his own greatness. Over the following years he worked with him and watched the horse come to dominate the race tracks throughout America; but there was one other winner he had never raced against, the elegant War Admiral. It was the middle of the 1930's depression when a race was fixed between the two horses and whole nation was caught up in the excitement of it. Charles S Howard told the jockey Red Pollard to let Seabiscuit run level with War Admiral until the first corner, where he was to pull him back and 'let him get a good look at him'. Once around the corner he was strap himself in and just let him go. What proceeded was one of the most adrenaline rushing pieces of racing that has ever taken place, as Seabiscuit thunders down the home straits in a comprehensive display of talent and speed.

After watching the race at least three times, we sat back in our chairs and my dad noted 'War Admiral was nicknamed Rear Admiral after that'.

That evening I decided to watch the race again on YouTube, then found myself flowing from one horse video to the next. Some taken by riders out hacking, some from eventers and others advertising horses for sale. I found particular delight in one piece of footage taken by a lady with a head camera who had decided to take a young four-year-old horse down to the beach. The beach had too many people on it for her to let it gallop and this horse was clearly over excited at the prospect, it took her all her time to hold him back from bolting. She managed to navigate it away from the beach and back along the sandy track, accompanied by lots of expletives as she was just about staying on board. At this moment the hedge in front of her jumps to life, as at least one hundred men dressed in camouflage gear continue their manoeuvres. This poor woman is having almost as much of a break down as her horse, so she quickly steers him back down the path onto the beach only to find a few moments later a Chinook helicopter landing in front of her. The footage goes blank at this point.

My father laughed almost as much as I did when I relayed the story to him.

There was something being kindled in the back of my mind, I had always loved horses and had had a brief dalliance as a teenager spending many a happy hour at the local riding school. My friend and I would cycle down during the school holidays and help out in return for a quick ride. We are talking about the late 1970's now, when health and safety had not been invented, so there was no problem in thundering around fields with no helmet on, occasionally wearing a skirt and open toed sandals (they were a thing back then). I had no formal training and no real idea what I was doing, but whatever it was, it was huge fun. I could feel a sense of excitement growing as I considered the prospect of getting back in the saddle. This would be more than a welcome break from the endless heaviness of dealing with terminal sickness and just the tonic I needed.

A year earlier my friend Ria had asked if I would take riding lessons with her and I had gladly agreed. We took one lesson at an established riding school as they had a couple of free spots available that week, but it didn't progress any further as they never any spaces available whenever we enquired. I decided to send her a text

'Do you fancy taking some riding lessons with me?'
Within a few minutes the phone pinged 'Yes, absolutely'.

We did a bit of research, found another riding school with a great reputation and booked ourselves in for a private weekly lesson.

For a pair of mature ladies, we giggled like a pair of school girls all the way there, such was the excitement of finally doing this thing. We pulled into the narrow concrete car park which ran alongside the stable block and got out. The smell hits you like a wall, the smell of horses. A strange combination of horse sweat, horse urine and horse muck. My heart was racing at a hundred miles an hour, it was the first time I felt anxious about doing this. We registered at the small reception desk, walked round to the rows of shelves on which sat every size of hat imaginable. I tried not to think of how many sweaty heads these hats had been perched on and spent a good ten minutes figuring out which actually fitted without wobbling when I moved or cutting off the circulation to the top of my head. Then came the bit I was not expecting, we had been told which horse we would be riding at the reception desk and it was our job to collect the horse from the stable and walk it to the arena. I wandered down the stable block looking for Dudley and froze with terror in front of a stable with one of the largest horses I had ever seen. He stared at me with liquid black eyes. My heart was now thumping so loud I am sure it was on surround sound, I could feel my hands trembling and I could not take my eyes off him. I gave myself a short pep talk and slowly slid the stable door open. As I approached he moved towards me, I made a sharp turn and ran out. This was ridiculous. Again, I told myself to get it together and walked back in, with shaking hands collected the reins and we walked out. We walked down the aisle and out into the daylight in complete silence, with my eyes the size of a barn owls fixed on the entrance; we processed through the courtyard and into the arena without looking at him once.

Our riding instructor was waiting for us. Lizzy was small, dark haired and took no captives – straight talking, tough, made you feel safe in her hands and I loved her. She would always think ahead and had no problem in shouting for people to stop running or using a tractor near the arena if she thought there was the slightest possibility they might spook the horses. She relayed instructions and before we knew it we were sat in the saddle and walking around the ménage. I found myself transfixed on Dudley's head, watching where his ears went, what he was looking at and most of all trying to figure out if he was planning on doing anything stupid. Lizzy had seen it all before and took no time in taking hold of the situation; she gave us a series of exercises to help us focus on riding and so we spent the next hour walking around the arena trying to keep our backs straight, feeling for our seat bones in the saddle, checking our hand position and making sure our feet were placed just inside the stirrups with our heels down. When it was finished we dismounted and walked our ride back to the stable.

It may sound stupid, but it was completely exhilarating. We both felt on an emotional high, we had been scared stupid when we started, by the time the lesson had ended there was a huge sense of accomplishment.

"Let's stop at Costa and have a drink" said Ria

We decided that we would get a loyalty card as we had every intention of making this a weekly event, even though we would need to drink what seemed like two hundred coffees before we both got a free one, we figured it would probably take us that long before we had learned to ride anyway.

And so it continued, each week we would drive to the stables, collect our horses and continue our education. Lizzy was always endlessly frustrated that I would perch forward and spent most of the lesson telling me to sit back. Whilst Ria got admonished for not pushing her horse on, as she was riding the reliable yet very switched on Molly, who knew full well that novice riders rarely have the balls to insist a horse does anything. If she remained in walk or only trotted around half

Dudley

the ménage instead of all of it, Ria would let her. Dudley was a completely different proposition and I soon grew to love him. If you told him to go – he went. He would happily gather quite a pace and to my surprise I found I really liked it. In fact, as the weeks went by and my confidence began to grow, the faster we went the happier I was. After a month or so we had progressed to canter and Lizzy decided that the next lesson would be a hack around the farm ride.

When I got home I mentioned to my husband that we would be out and about in the countryside the following week. He looked deeply concerned
"Isn't that dangerous?"
"Not really" I replied

This was not the reassuring answer he was looking for and decided that he was going to buy me a proper riding hat. Just in case.

We drove to the local saddlery, an amazing store packed to the rafters with goodies and grabbed the nearest assistant, who just happened to be the manager.

"I want you fit my wife with a good strong hat and I don't care what it costs" announced Phil.

Her eyes lit up and she promptly stopped what she was doing and gave me her undivided attention. I stood there while she plonked one hat after another on my head, obligingly shaking my head, or looking at my feet when she asked me to. After nearly an hour she felt that we had arrived at the perfect fit for me, a Charles Owen 4 star hat. This is no ordinary hat – I could go eventing in this little baby and be fine. Phil stood at the till wide eyed when she casually announced that the hat was over two hundred pounds. Well, he had offered...

The following week we arrived at the stables in a ball of excitement, in fact we were so early for our lesson we had nearly an hour to spare. I now had my own riding hat, I had no need to search through shelves trying to find one, so it took us no time at all to grab our horses and be stood ready for Lizzy. I was pleased that I had Dudley, I felt relaxed with him. Ria however, was less than relaxed as she had been assigned a horse that she had not ridden before and looked deeply worried as we waited to depart. Luca was a small piebald cob, a chunky compact little pony who looked as surprised to find himself stood outside as Ria was to find herself sat on him. Lizzy eventually arrived on her own horse and off we walked. With her years of experience, she talked us through everything, told us when to stop our horses to let them look at something so they wouldn't spook, to sit back when we went down the track towards the river and forwards as we climbed back up. We only had one small event as a rabbit darted out of the bushes and Luca had a little jump sideways, thankfully Ria managed to stay in the saddle. We finally came to a small hill which we could canter up if we wanted to. I was immediately excited to try it and Ria reluctantly agreed as well. Lizzy set off and we all followed. Dudley soon found his stride and raced behind Lizzy with absolute joy. It was all over in minutes, but I loved it.

"Can we do it again?" I pleaded

"No" came Lizzy's firm reply

"Please"

"No"

Sat in Costa later we sat scanning our phones looking at horses for sale and dreaming about houses with stables, paddocks, the works. It is fair to say, we were hooked.

As the months went by I began to imagine what it would be like to own my own horse. It was easy to spend the whole evening on the iPad looking at horses for sale and trying to decide which one I would pick. I had no idea what any of the terms meant and it as quite a shock when Ria explained that a horse doing a novice test had nothing to do with being suitable for a novice rider. The more I read, the more I realised that there is a whole world of 'horse language' which I knew nothing about. Ria was very good at explaining so many things to me, she knew so much about horses that I could quite happily chat to her for hours. Although she was new to riding her daughter had ridden from a very early age. She had already owned a succession of horses and their current charge was a warmblood mare who seemed to be more injury prone that the entire Premier league football squad. On top of all the leg and back injuries, most requiring surgery, there was an endless parade of small, almost comical stuff – she had hay fever, asthma, was allergic to her own sweat and couldn't be left out in the rain. She was moody, temperamental and skittish – but they loved her to bits. I guess, in this mare's defence, she was gorgeous to look at with long elegant legs and she could do an exceptional dressage test when she was in the mood.

We would often find ourselves at the yard doing some quick job or other and I was more than happy to help out. Things had become a little more intense for Ria in recent weeks, as the mare had reared up when she was being brought back from the paddock and landed on the handler breaking her leg. From that point on, the yard refused to handle her, so Ria and her daughter found themselves there four times a day. Turning out, bringing in, meal time feeds and night time checks. We were on our way back from Costa when we saw the sky turn black before us and Ria asked

"Would you mind if we went straight to the yard to put the horse in?"

"Of course not" I replied.

By the time we got there the rain had started and all the horses seemed very jittery. Ria grabbed a carrot and a head collar, and we made our way to the paddock as quickly as we could. Just as we approached the final gate the lightening started. We both stood there for a moment, our fear was palpable; we could see the mare looking anxious and knew we had yet to somehow get her back to the stable with the strong possibility that the lightning would strike causing her to do who knows what. I looked at Ria and she said 'let's go' – so she marched into the field towards the horse while I stood holding the handle of the electric fence ready to open it when she got close. She watched Ria approach staring directly at the carrot in her outstretched hand, when the mare took the carrot in one deft movement the head collar was on and Ria was striding back towards the gate with the horse in tow. They made their way through the gate and headed down the path as the next bolt of lightning struck. To our amazement the mare did nothing, but I suddenly became aware that I was stood in a field holding a wire containing an electrical current in a lightning storm. That would be truly ironic, after listening to all the lectures from hubby on the dangers of horse riding, if I actually met my demise not from some nasty fall but by being frazzled by a fatal lightning/electric fence combination. In a flash the handle was back in place and I hastened my way after Ria, who by this time had successfully marched the mare into her stable and she was now propped against the wall breathing for the first time in ten minutes.

"That was close" she muttered.

Agreed.

Ria had spent the last ten years around horses, she knew everything there was to know and had a healthy respect for how unpredictable they could be. Together we made a great pair, we spurred each other on and when we did inevitably fall off, encouraged each other to get 'back into the saddle'. My first fall came when we were cantering down the long side of the arena and my foot came out of one of the stirrups.

In slow motion, I slid sideways out of the saddle and onto the floor with Dudley stopping as soon as he felt me go. I was not injured in any way, just felt daft that I had come off in front of a class full of people.

Ria's fall was much worse. She had signalled to canter at the corner, gone to grab the saddle strap for safety at the same time the horse turned. She flew off and hit the ground hard, hurting her shoulder and back and putting her out of action for weeks. Physical injuries may soon heal, but the dent to your confidence takes some getting past. Fear makes you retreat from things, it robs you of joy and conjures up a thousand pictures of nasty and horrible 'what-ifs'. For years I have watched my mother-in-law respond to every situation with fear, utterly convinced that whatever the worst possible outcome could be, that would be the one that would happen. She saw her father die of TB when she was young and afterwards had been the main breadwinner for the family until her siblings were old enough to look after themselves. She had faced a horrific circumstance, but then that one event became the block on which she built the rest of her life. It occurred to me many years ago that we all have a choice when shit happens to us, we let it in, or we choose to take it on headfirst.

I was finding myself in a pretty shitty situation now. The shock of my father's illness had passed and now we were in the relentless decline, with the constant demands that brings. I had spent the day at my parents' house and was on my way home one evening when the phone rang, and my mother was desperate for me to come straight back

"Your father has had a fall and can't get up. You have to come back"

I turned the car around and forty minutes later walked back into the house to find my father lay on the floor unable to move. I tried with every ounce of strength within me to lift him, but I just couldn't manage it. Eventually I phoned Phil, who drove down and got him back into the chair. What hit me most from that evening was the sadness in my father's eyes, he was a proud and independent man who found it utterly humiliating to be so helpless. It is moments like those which take the biggest emotion toll, the complete hopelessness you feel, as no matter how hard you try, the deterioration is constant, merciless and there is not a thing you can do about it.

The following morning I sat on the sofa watching the sun rise through the open window. As the daylight slowly crept up through the branches of the trees, I felt a growing determination that I was not going to sink but find a way to keep my spirits buoyant. The more I toyed with the idea, the more I realised that the happy point in every week was the horse riding. I felt alive and exhilarated after every lesson and spent the whole week reliving the joy of every moment. In a flash I made the decision that I would look around for a horse that was available for loan. I had seen adverts from owners wanting people to ride their horses a couple of times a week in return for a small payment and a helping hand, so I knew this was something that could be explored. After trawling through the adverts for loaners one thing was crystal clear, nobody wanted a novice rider anywhere near their horse. So, it was by chance that on responding to one advert I was directed to a lady who had a small stable with a few liveries and an old mare called Megan who needed hacking out twice a week. This chestnut thoroughbred was in her twenties, had seen it all and I was assured was supremely safe. It was a great arrangement. I could hack her out with the group as long as I mucked out the stable and filled the haynets and water buckets.

I arrived bright and early on the first morning, a crisp Sunday in February. Only the yard owner was around and apologised profusely that she was still in her dressing gown

"really, it's OK, I am miles too early" I replied.

I liked her, she had a warm and easy manner, quite happily welcoming a whole host of people on to the small yard at the back of her house. The cottage was a beautiful farmhouse and the stables were built from mellow Cheshire brick. Beyond the stables there were a couple of fields for grazing, the muck heap which was more like a muck mountain and the sand ménage.

This was quite a big step for me, I was here without Ria and about to ride a horse that was unfamiliar to me. I entered the stable and stood next to Megan who was busy munching hay. She was huge, possibly seventeen hands high and towered above me. But there was something about her manner which made me feel relaxed in her company. We spent the next forty minutes together, while I groomed and chatted, and she ate. The next step was tacking up. By now quite a few people had arrived and I could hear the sound of voices and horses' hooves as they were being brought out of their various stables to be made ready for a hack. I pottered down to the tack room, said a few hellos on my way, collected Megan's tack and made my way back to her stable. Once inside I was desperately hoping that I could tack this horse up without having to ask for help. In all the months I had been taking lessons at the riding school I had always arrived at a horse who was already saddled and ready to go. The saddlecloth and the saddle seemed pretty straightforward. The bridle was a whole different story, this flimsy set of straps flopped everywhere and no amount of playing about seemed to make any sense at all. In the end I had to resort to asking the lady in the neighbouring stable if she could help me and within ten seconds she had the bridle on and stood looking at me with a quizzical expression on her face.

"It's not the same as the one I'm used to" I mumbled. To which she left looking even more puzzled than before.

We all assembled in the main yard and in turn mounted our horses using a workman's bench as a mounting block. Our body of horses then moved on mass through the gate, down the drive at the side of the house and off down the road. Hacking with these ladies became a very pleasurable experience, they were friendly, chatty and good humoured. Megan was a delight. I had been told that in every circumstance I should let Megan do her thing, as she would always look after me; so that was how it was, I sat there being transported by the ginger giant without any fear at all. She walked sensibly along with the group, looked at odd objects but nothing more and had a gorgeous trot. The only thing which I found disappointing was the lack of off road riding. I had imagined that we would have the odd opportunity to have a canter through a field or on a bridle path, but there were none locally, so we were left just walking around roads on one of three circuits.

After a couple of weeks, I was approached by another one of the liveries asking if I was interested in loaning her horse. This was an intriguing prospect, as the horse was younger, so I could practice cantering in the ménage. I agreed and the loan was to begin the following week. The day arrived and as usual I arrived bright and early, said hello to Megan and approached Woody's stable to find the owner already there.

"I'd like to run through the jobs I want you to do and how I would like you to do them" she announced.

Fair enough. We began with the bedding, she was only going to use one bag of shavings a week, so I had to make it last. This was the point when I was introduced to the art of muck flicking. You take scoop of shavings onto your fork, toss it in the air, let the shavings fall to the floor while catching the poo on your fork. It's quite a skill – if you toss them too high they go everywhere; too low and nothing happens. Skilled muck flickers can complete a stable in about ten minutes. I found it was taking me closer to an hour and I would always emerge into the daylight looking like I'd been flocked.

Then there was the food, Woody was fed twice a day; although I was not quite sure why. This little cob was chunky to say the least but this lovely old lady treated him as her adored pet so there was no possibility that he would be allowed to go hungry, he had two hefty meals and hay on tap.

After all the jobs, grooming and guided tour of the tack was completed, we made our way to the ménage for my first ride on Woody. We were joined by the groom and they stood next to the fence while I walked Woody into the ménage and got mounted. What followed has to be one of the best examples of how not to treat a new rider – both the owner and the groom began shouting instructions like a verbal machine gun on rapid fire; 'sit back', 'tighten the reins' 'don't pull at the mouth' 'close your fingers' and on and on. After only ten minutes in trot, this poor little pony was virtually foaming at the mouth and covered in sweat. It was clearly over for this session, so I dismounted and we all lined back across the field with the pony in tow. I drove home feeling pretty low. I knew I was a learner, but surely common sense would tell you that you are not going to help someone improve by simply shouting at them. The following week went pretty much the same way as the first and I was beginning to feel pretty downhearted about the whole experience. The third week brought a lucky break, the owner had an appointment which she had to keep, so I had Woody all to myself. After the jobs were completed I walked him to the ménage and we had a play, first a walk, then a trot and then into canter. This pony seemed absolutely thrilled to be cantering around and went at it with all the energy he could muster. After a circuit round I was getting to grips with how to ride it, I wasn't bouncing around so much and was able to sit in the saddle and ride into the movement. After fifteen minutes it was clear that the pony was pooped, so I let him stretch his neck, then walked him back to the stable; both of us seemed delighted with our mornings exertions.

Out of nowhere came another one of the loan ladies 'Gosh isn't he covered in sweat, what have you been doing with him?"

Now I have been around to know when someone is trouble and she was ringing all my bells. I had to put up with her constantly interfering in everything I did, usually with a sentence beginning '"well, I wouldn't let him do that", so I was not that surprised to be pulled aside by the owner the following week to be told that I couldn't ride Woody for a few weeks and when I did it would only be in the ménage under her supervision and nothing else. I suspected that something had been said, but when I asked why, she shuffled about saying the saddle fitter had been out and Woody's saddle didn't fit properly. I have no idea whether that was the real reason, but this was becoming too much of a drama for ten minutes in the saddle, so I called it a day.

My next loan was just as short. Having responded to an advertisement in the local equine centre I now found myself meeting an inspiring pensioner, full of beans, with the most remarkable take on life. She owned a feisty grey called Ben, with whom she had the most amazing relationship. He had so many tumours around his head that wearing a conventional bridle was impossible, so she took herself off to a Parelli master class and bought a Parelli bridle which looked for all the world like a thin bit of rope to me. There seemed to be no apparent way she could control this horse, yet they operated beautifully together.

"I believe you are interested in loaning Ben?" I said, stroking this inquisitive grey gelding.

"Oh yes, but that's Ben. It's Big Ben we want to loan." As she said this, the ground shook slightly, the sun was eclipsed by the frame of one of the largest horses I had ever seen. "This is Big Ben." No kidding.

Our first outing was pleasant enough. Big Ben took his confidence from the grey and seemed very happy to be out and about stretching his legs. He had a gorgeous rhythmic trot and was very responsive to my instruction. If I moved in the saddle to indicate a faster gait he quickly obliged, and if I sat back, he would slow down. I was enjoying him a lot. It was only toward the end of our first hack that the reason for the loan became clear. The real owner was quite frightened of riding him, as he could spook. His *modus operandi* was a 'full spin' and a possible jump for good measure.

"Don't worry," said the pensioner "If he spins, just sit back and keep your feet pressed down into the stirrups."

Up to that point, I had not been the slightest bit bothered about riding him, but this new information was a game changer. The next few days I thought a lot about what she had told me but decided that I had seen no evidence, so I would give it another go. Now here is where this fear thing kicks in – it was the same horse and the same route we had taken last time, but now I was frightened. And the further we hacked, the more frightened I became. So did Big Ben. Things which we had happily passed last week were catching his eye and he was suddenly trotting or moving of his own accord, taking me with him. I could feel his nerves and at points he was shaking. I became terrified - we were literally egging each other on in a stupid game of Who Is Going to Freak Out First. I have never been so glad to get off a horse in my life. Thankfully, when I phoned that evening to explain why I would not be continuing, she did understand.

I began to feel that horse loans were not going to work for me. I was busy discussing this with Ria and her daughter Chrissy as we drove to see her mare, when Chrissy asked me directly "Caroline, why don't you just buy your own horse?"

I sat for a moment, then in an instant decided that was exactly what I was going to do.

Big Ben

Chapter Two

The months laboured on as I looked after my ever-failing father, it was torturous to watch such a proud and well-built man diminish in front of my eyes. His sight began to fail him, and his spirits were sinking. More than ever, I looked forward to the escape of riding and the prospect of buying my own horse. This was the shot of energy I needed, and I threw myself into a horse purchase with all the dedication of a zealot monk. No website, Facebook page or notice board escaped my attention. I spotted a beautiful black cob who was eight years old and had 'been used to teach a novice to ride', he sounded perfect.

Accompanied by Ria's daughter Chris, we headed off to Leeds to view him. It was one of those wet afternoons with a fine rain that wasn't sufficient to prevent you from doing anything, but it did ensure all your hair and clothes were thoroughly drenched by the time you had finished. The horse was being sold by a dealer, who walked us to the stable and introduced a pony which looked considerably smaller than the advertised 15 hands. He cowered at the back of his stable and positively jumped out of his skin when one of the neighbouring stable doors blew shut. My heart went out to him, he looked scared and disorientated. I knew he wasn't going to be right for me, but we had driven an hour to see him, so we were going to give him a proper chance. He was tacked up and walked out to the exercise arena, so after everyone else had ridden him, I got on. He had moved about at the mounting block trying to stop me from mounting but went at a steady pace when we did get going. He pottered along quite happily until we got to the second corner where a pile of jump poles lay on the floor. He made a decided swerve and cut out the entire corner to avoid them. The same thing happened again on the third corner when he spotted a water bucket. Although he was sweet and very handsome, on the way home we concluded that he was a touch too small and potentially too much of a 'spooker' for me.

On a roll, I booked the next viewing for the following week. I had spotted a mare brought over from Ireland where she had been used for trekking. Again, I had Chris acting as my trusty advisor and after nearly an hour we arrived at a Darling Buds of May homestead. The paintwork was a worn Cheshire red, with mellow orange bricks and a perfectly welcoming atmosphere. We were greeted by a rotund, vivacious blonde who bubbled away the entire walk from the car to the stable.

"And here she is," she announced gaily as we stood staring at what must be one of the ugliest horses I have ever seen. She was a mottled clay colour with a disproportionately large neck and what my mother would call, a 'mincey walk'.

"She's not been blessed with beauty," I observed. There was a stilted silence and I looked round to be met by a steely glare from Chris. She told me later that you must never tell anyone their horse is ugly, it's like insulting someone's baby. Lesson learned.

This horse certainly had a pleasant manner but clearly didn't like doing anything more than she absolutely had to. After a brief hack down the lane, we tried her out in the ménage. She had no intention of doing anything for me and felt as heavy as lead when she did move.

"Well, what do you want?" inquired the blonde. "This is a novice ride as you can see. She won't go if you don't ride her properly, so she's super safe." But she then completed her otherwise nonsensical sentence by saying something which had a profound ring of truth to it.

"People should buy the horses for where they are now and not where they want to be."

She worked very hard to get us to commit, like so many dealers, their interest is a financial one, they need to sell the horse to earn their commission. Her final play was a diatribe about a family who were coming to view the mare tomorrow and bringing a saddle, so I shouldn't expect her to be here tomorrow evening if I don't grab her now. What she didn't realise was that I was quite happy for the family with the saddle to take her.

My next viewing was an impulse one. It didn't take long to realise that everyone wanted the same thing – a safe, sensible horse that had some life experience, who would look after its rider. I lost count of the number of calls I made for horses that had been advertised only that day to find out they had already been viewed and a deposit left. Then when I saw a black cob who had been in the same family for the last five years, safe, sensible with plenty of experience so I jumped at it. No one was available to view him with me, so I went on my own literally that afternoon. As soon as I saw him I fell in love, there was something there with this one that had been missing with all the others – a connection. I rode him in the ménage and he formed a beautiful outline, but nerves got the better of me and I decided not to canter on him. He was perfect.

Now this is where having someone with some knowledge with you makes all the difference. When I asked if there were any health issues, the owner disclosed that he had hay fever and this resulted in headshaking in the summer months. For those of you who know anything about headshaking, you will probably be headshaking yourselves about now. For those of you who don't, as I subsequently learned, headshaking occurs when the highly sensitive sensors in a horse's nose fire a signal similar to a bee sting whenever they are triggered by a stimulus, and for this horse, the stimulus was pollen. Being as naïve as I was, I went home, googled horse hay fever and it didn't seem like such a big problem. I placed a sizeable deposit and then went on my planned holiday where I spent the whole week on a blissful cloud of happiness. On my return, everything was in lock down – the vetting was due that week and we had the livery set up and travel details secured.

The bubble burst mid-afternoon the day before the vetting was due. I received a call from one of the practice partners who had been preparing for the vetting he was conducting the following day and was deeply concerned at my disclosure of 'head-shaking'. He firmly told me that he could not endorse the purchase of a horse with any form of headshake. While the symptoms may be mild now, they can progress to an extent which will make the horse dangerous to ride and impossible to sell. He confirmed this again in more detail in a long email later that evening. Not wanting to believe this, I phoned a local, well-respected Equine Centre of Excellence and asked for their opinion. The response was the same.

"There are plenty of other horses out there, go and find one of those. I have seen enough heartbroken owners when their horses have to be put to sleep not to wish that on anyone."

I fell into an empty, dark pit of despair, literally in a couple of hours my energy disappeared, and it seemed like nothing would ever go right. On top of that, I had to tell the owner I was no longer proceeding with the purchase. I picked up the phone and her warm greeting soon turned into despairing outrage.

"What's to become of him then? Is he going to be put down now as something worthless?"

I certainly didn't have the answer, but seemingly by the following morning she did. I received an email saying that she was mistaken, and he didn't headshake and she would be cross if I said he did. Furthermore, she would not be returning my deposit. We battled on for several months until we finally settled on a refund of half the deposit. Another painful lesson learned.

After a short respite, I resumed the hunt. I was now becoming to understand some of the terms used in adverts, but better yet, exactly what they implied.

Genuine : generally not much trouble

Sensitive mouth : needs only the lightest touch to change direction. Club hands beware

Forward going : kick too hard and you will be doing 0-30 in under ten seconds

Forward going but safe : may eventually stop

Scopey jump : if the jump is 50cm you will be jumping a metre

Needs a confident rider : super spooky, expect to hit the deck on your first hack

Has been on a farm ride : has been ridden once around a field

Has seen a tractor : probably over the fence of his field

Green/needs bringing on : knows nothing, so unless you do, you are in deep doo-doo

If the advert doesn't mention that the horse is good to load or catch, then expect to add a minimum of forty minutes onto any planned outing to allow for you running around a field trying to get hold of him and then the general circling and coaxing required to get him into the horsebox.

We were now into summer and good horses were snapped up as soon as they were advertised. My daughter's friend Sia, who had the foresight to major in Equine Science, was enrolled in the search. At 10 p.m. one evening she spotted a newly placed advert for a schoolmaster cob close to where she was based in London and made an appointment to view it at 9 a.m. the following morning. While she was trying him out, a further two potential buyers showed up and one placed her ten-year-old daughter in the saddle quite literally as soon as Sia vacated it. Sia phoned me and although I hadn't seen him I trusted her judgement, so between us we agreed to buy the horse there and then and informed the dealer. We asked for her bank details, so I could send through the deposit and then arrange for the vetting.

"Sure, no problem," she said. Yet by five o'clock that evening I had not received a text and was unable to get any response to my calls, so I wasn't wholly surprised when she eventually phoned me to tell me she had sold the horse to the lady with the young daughter as she was paying cash, did not want a vetting as she was taking the horse there and then.

I won't run through every horse I viewed, only the two which had a profound effect on my confidence and shook me up quite considerably. My first was with a dealer in Brighton, a good five hours drive from my home. By the time I arrived, after being held up in several traffic jams, it was one o'clock and I was tired and dehydrated.

I had seen several video clips of the horse and he looked amazing, a beautiful 15'2 hands high, hogged cob, glossy black with full feathers and a thick flowing tail. He moved with grace and had a considerable jump. I was introduced to him and the young female dealer then disappeared to find some tack saying, "I'll leave you to say hello."

'Well hello," I said, whilst leaning over the stable door. The horse then moved towards me and bit me on the arm. I knew there and then I didn't like him, but I had spent over six hours in the car driving to see him, so I would see it through. Once in the saddle, he was very responsive and what I was soon to discover, had a very sensitive mouth. The slightest movement of the reins would cause him to make a very definite change in direction. I had done a few laps of the ménage in trot and decided to ask for canter at the corner, but I realise now that I must have pulled on the inside rein as we suddenly went into a full spin. We shot round and round and all I could see were the flashing hooves below me and I was utterly convinced I was going to fall onto them.

When we eventually stopped, I was completely shell-shocked and just sat there stunned. Seeing this the dealer quickly pulled the horse out of the ménage and before I had the chance to collect my thoughts or get off she was jumping on her own horse and we were heading off across the fields for a hack.

"You really need to see him out and about'" she quipped gaily.

Still very wary, I sat perched on the saddle, trying to maintain a steady breath while we hacked past mountains of plastic rubbish, a bonfire and a discarded canoe, all things known to spook horses. This one really didn't bother at all, so I began to relax.

"There, I told you he was brilliant" said the dealer and in fairness to him, he was.

We finished the hack with a gentle trot down the road, where I got into trouble again. Seasoned pros can hold the reins without their hands moving a single inch, novice riders really can't. This became very apparent as we zigzagged down the road, narrowly missing cars and vans. When we eventually got back to the yard, I got off and went, feeling desperately unhappy all the way home.

After another respite caused by both a crisis of confidence and my father's ever deteriorating condition, I decided to give it another go. I had already decided that I was not going to travel across the country in search of a horse, nothing more than an hour's drive from home. So, accompanied by Sia who had kindly travelled up from London for the day and my husband, we trundled over to a local dealer who had 'the perfect novice ride' for me to view. This piebald mare seemed happy enough to be stroked, but we were slightly concerned that her ears remained pinned back the entire time, which felt unnerving.

We undertook the now very familiar parade to the ménage, and I use this word as a very loose description of the circle of sand in the corner of the field, with an old wicker chair as a mounting block. To add to the irony, the dealer rode the horse while the viewing party had to wade through two feet of sludgy mud behind her. My prized Ariat riding boots were caked in the stuff, unbelievable. Both the dealer and Sia rode the mare and then it was my turn. She walked without any problem but would only trot for a few steps before falling back into a walk again. "Here," said the dealer, "try this,"' and handed me a schooling whip. As soon as the whip was in my grasp the horse suddenly started off in full bolt, with me holding on for dear life. Round and round we went, with her head clearly set towards the fence on the final turn she looked as though she was going to try and jump it. Somehow, I must have loosened the reins or moved the crop out of her eye line, she slowed, then stopped. I quite literally jumped off. Although I felt relatively fine at the time, it was afterwards that the whole incident began to play on my mind. What if she had jumped and I had fallen off, I could have broken my neck. What the hell was I doing even thinking of buying a horse, when clearly, I had no idea how to control one.

Beautiful, but too much for me to handle

One of the dealers I had encountered on my journey told me that it wasn't how well you could ride, but whether you could ride confidently. She said that many horses were ridden by poor riders, but those riders had the confidence to insist the horse do what they wanted and that was all that mattered. Well, my confidence was shot to bits. Even the smell of horses at the riding school would send my heart racing and my mind into panic mode. I bought a body protector the size of a boiler cover and wore it to every lesson. I wouldn't canter for weeks and would only ride two horses who I knew were the safest in the yard.

It was now July 2016 and we were entering the final stage of my father's life. He was admitted to hospital after he suffered a stroke, and for weeks, my sister and I would take turns sitting by his bedside. During that time, he would be awake for a couple of hours during the day, otherwise he slept. I had discovered the Intelligent Horsemanship website and ordered three books by Kelly Marks, which I diligently read during those long days. There was an exercise that intrigued me involving picturing an event and running through that event again and again in your mind, playing it exactly how you would like it to happen. As a professional jockey at the time, Kelly described a race she was entered in and how she practiced in her mind being on the horse, competing in that race and storming past the finishing line first. You probably won't be surprised to learn that when the race eventually did take place, she won with ease.

Kelly even described how she had dealt with historic events, things which had happened years ago which had knocked her confidence. She had replayed them in her mind picturing a different, better outcome – until the better version became the more real of the two for her. I used the technique and found that I was able to change my mind-set about the events that had frightened me. I no longer felt like my confidence was gone, but that I was a confident, if somewhat inexperienced rider.

The final few days of my father's time in hospital were without doubt the worst for all of us. It was clear that he was nearing the end, so palliative care arranged for us to have our own room on the stroke ward, with a small bed for one of us to sleep in, so we could stay with him. We spent days in a constant cycle – my father would suddenly struggle to breathe and want morphine to relax his muscles. This had been no problem at home, as we had small vials which could be given as soon as he needed them. Now we were in hospital every dose turned into a twenty-minute drama, the nurse had to be called, she then had to get the doctor who needed a second person to go with him and duel sign the release of the drug. The nurse would then be advised she could administer it and would eventually show up vial in hand. By this time my father would have worked himself into a small frenzy and the stress of trying to calm him down when he was squirming in his bed gasping for breath was horrendous. After two days with hardly any sleep and the episodes getting more and more frequent I became desperate for help. By the time the palliative care team turned up I was pretty mad, it seemed ridiculous that there wasn't a way of keeping my father's condition monitored and him free of pain. It transpires that there was a way, but no one had thought to apply it yet. Within the hour the necessary kit arrived, so now a cocktail of morphine and relaxants were administered by constant feed which thankfully put a stop to the peaks when dad was desperately fighting for breath.

My sister and I took it in turns to stay with him. One of us would stay all day and night swopping over in the morning when the other arrived to pick up their shift. The night time was always difficult, it was a baking hot July and I found myself lay on a bed with a plastic cover; overheated, restless and unable to sleep. Quite apart from the constant noise from around the ward, I found myself tuned into dad's breathing. I would suddenly start in bed, realising that must have drifted off and I hadn't heard anything for a while. The outside lights in the car park gave a dim glow which worked its way under the gap in the curtains, allowing me to see just enough that I could check my father's chest was still moving up and down. It was like playing Russian Roulette, as the days went by we knew that either my sister or I would be on the watch when the end finally came.

I had finished my shift, had a lovely day out with Phil and was in bed when the phone rang at midnight that evening, it was my sister

"You'd better come now"

Without asking anything more I raced to the hospital and into our room. She was stood by the bed next to dad who lay stretched out and lifeless. The sudden shock of seeing him broke in me like a tsunami of emotion and I collapsed in tears. I cried solidly for four days, great big, heartfelt, wrenching, sob-out-loud crying. Even though we had seen this time coming for quite some time, nothing actually prepares you for the finality of it all. And how so many of your memories and so much of your identity and shared history is inextricably tied to the person you will never have the chance to sit with or talk to again. I felt so guilty that I had ever actually wished it would all end during the winter months when every day brought fresh battles with doctors, caregivers and struggles over pain relief or meal replacements. Well, now it had, and I would have given anything to have him back.

I still miss him so much

Chapter Three

Grief works in funny ways and I think it is probably different for everyone. During the first few weeks I had uncontrollable emotions, I cried that much my eyes hurt. My sister was calm and collected, yet I knew her well enough to know that she was feeling things as very deeply indeed.

"I just can't cry" she would confide
"I think I'm crying enough for both of us" I replied

Phil told me that he felt almost detached from emotion when his father died, and I know he didn't cry either, which would seem odd to anyone who knew how close they both were. It was nearly a year later when he was driving back from a business meeting that 'And I miss you' played on the radio and all the grief came flooding out. He had to pull into a lay-by and just sat there crying. The same thing happened to my sister, it was months later when the grief took hold and she let it all flow out.

When things end, there is a point when you then start to think about the future, you are ready to move forward. I decided to give myself permission to start to let go, I had given it my all when it was needed, but things had now changed, and I could change with them. Mother was fine, we had a system of carers in place and of course, still lots of support from my sister and I. But this was a different journey, a settled and maintainable one.

Phil had decided that a holiday was required and that September he found a gorgeous, all-inclusive hotel in Tenerife and off we went. It turned out to be just what we needed, away from the everyday and in the glorious sunshine, things felt possible again. The future was out there and ready to be explored. Obviously for me, the future was definitely horse shaped. During the day, I would idle away my time clicking through Horsequest to see if there was anything that looked right for me. And boom – there he was. A stunning 14'2 hands high grey Highland cob cross who had, at eleven, been there and done it. There was just something about him that kept drawing me back to him. I tried contacting the owner, but the signal was so poor I couldn't get through. I resigned myself that he would probably be sold by the time we got back from our holiday. The only saving grace was that he was based in the backend of Cornwall, so you either lived locally or had to be really interested to want to travel all the way down there to see him. My resolution of only viewing locally would be blown to bits, this horse was the farthest yet, over six hours drive away.

I called again as soon as we got home, to be told that they had received lots of inquiries, but the distance had presented a problem for viewings. I was now very proficient at pre-viewing questions after being misled as many times as I had, there were no bases I wouldn't be prepared to cover. All seemed well, the only slight concern was the fact that they had only had him for six months. Both parents were keen horse people and he had been bought for their teenage daughter, but after the initial peak she had showed little interest and, in fact, had only ridden him a handful of times all summer. They were reluctantly selling him, as they could see no point in keeping him if she was not going to ride him. The previous owner, again a teenager, had owned him from the age of four and she was very keen to be kept in the loop with where he was and what he was up to.

A small piece of serendipity now kicked in. My sister and her husband had already made the summer long pilgrimage to their caravan in Cornwall, so I rang her.

"How far are you from Bodmin Moor?" I asked. It turned out they were literally twenty minutes' drive from the place where the horse was based. So, it was finalised, we would view the horse and spend the weekend with them.

For the rest of the week I spent every spare minute mentally journeying through my viewing. What it would feel like, how I would take my time, what moves I would try and how glorious he would be. That same bubble of excitement returned, and I knew that it was going to be a great viewing. I drove my husband down to our hotel that Friday night in record time. We were staying about ten minutes from the livery yard, but I still made him get up at the crack of dawn, consume breakfast at lightening pace and be bundled into the car nearly an hour before we were due to arrive.

This actually worked out to be an inspired move, as sat navs have a wholly different idea of where a place actually is when you use them in Cornwall. We found ourselves crawling down dirt tracks with old stone walls and sky-high bramble hedges that make your teeth grind as they scratch your car when you pass. Then, onto duel carriageways before again plummeting into the undergrowth in the faint hope that the little arrow on the screen actually had some idea of where we were supposed to be going. Eventually, and unbelievably ten minutes late, we arrive at a small family livery in the middle of Bodmin Moor. We were greeted by the owner, an instantly likeable lady with a great sense of humour and an open and honest demeanour. The couple who owned the horse were also there, although quieter by nature, they were warm, welcoming and struck me as decent people.

After what seemed like a lifetime of pleasantries, we were invited to walk out to the field to see him. As we entered the field he looked up, acknowledged us and then carried on eating.

Pudding

He was a glorious white which shone in the sunshine and he had almost a saintly glow to him. My heart was racing at a hundred miles an hour, I so desperately wanted him to be the right horse. He made no attempt to run away and stood quietly while we placed the head collar on. So this was Pudding. He was absolutely gorgeous, radiating a certain air of calm and kindness and I was already completely taken in by him. As we walked together back to the yard, he seemed altogether at peace with life, as though nothing bothered him. I groomed him and picked out his feet and we tacked him up. It's funny how some horses make you very wary, but this fella inspired confidence; so far everything felt perfect.

I somehow knew my sister wouldn't want to be left out. She knew how much this meant to me and she is the kind of person that it would now mean a lot to her. So sure enough, just before we began to ride, both her and her husband pulled up. This was absolutely perfect. I couldn't somehow imagine, after all we had been through in the last eighteen months, anything better than her being part of this.

After the number of close calls, I had had with other horses when I had viewed them, I knew that it was vital I detached my emotions and be as level headed as possible. It had been arranged that Pudding would be ridden by someone before I got on, so one of the other liveries mounted for a demonstration ride. She had done one circuit of the ménage when someone on the neighbouring farm across the lane started a large hedge-cutter and Pudding jumped forwards to get away from the noise. I drew a short breath, please after all of this, don't let him be a spooky horse. A few more laps completed it was now my turn.

Pudding was a whole heap lazier than the pre-viewing videos had suggested. We spent a good twenty minutes just walking around – straight ahead, in circles, across and back again. Then the same circuit in trot. When I had built up enough nerve, we did get around to cantering and he had such a rhythmic rocking chair ride that was so much better than even I could have hoped for. So far so good. It was then decided that we would now take him out and about.

"Do you want to take him on your own?" enquired the owner.

This completely baffled me

"I have no idea where I am going" I replied
"Oh, sorry no, I mean, do you want us to take another horse out with you, or just accompany you on our bikes so you can see he's ok on his own"
"I'm fine with another horse" I replied.

They then brought the husband's horse out of the stable. He was magnificent looking beast, originally bought for the wife but he had proved to be too much of a white-knuckle ride for her to enjoy, so now the husband rode him. Once tacked up we set off, the slow decent down the cobbled path to the lane and a steady walk down the lane to the moor. Behind us was a small convoy, the wife on her bicycle and behind her in the car was my sister and the rest of my party who had decided to return to the hotel to wait for me there. We said goodbye at the top of the lane and I continued behind the thoroughbred, actually quite some distance behind. Pudding was a plodder and had no intention of being bullied into action by the striding gait of his companion, we would get there in our own good time thank you very much. Eventually we reached the entrance to the moor. It was a glorious day, with greenery as far as the eye could see and a huge cloudless sky. There was a warm gentle breeze and the sounds of nature all around us. We lost the wife as soon as we left the narrow track as the moor was unsuitable terrain for a bike, so the horses ventured on together, well not completely together as the husband trotted on leaving Pudding and I alone; enjoying the moment. We passed Longhorn cattle, herds of wild ponies and Pudding didn't bat an eyelid. My main job, really, was to keep him from stopping to eat. We came to a stream and let the horses wade in and take a drink, then back onto the strip of road which dissected the moor. A few cars and a tractor passed, which didn't bother Pudding one jot. After about an hour, we returned back to the yard and my heart was set on him. I felt better on him than I had on any of the other horses I had tried. This was the one.

I helped untack, watch him get showered off and fed, then I headed back to the hotel almost an hour later than we had anticipated. My brother-in-law was under the impression that the main reason we were down there was to 'see' Cornwall, so when I eventually met back up with them he was keen for us to 'get going'. We spent the afternoon visiting their favourite beach, walking along cliff tops and the evening getting ever so merry in a local seafood restaurant. My mind, however, was never far from that wonderful little horse and the amazing sense of happiness I was feeling.

Bright and early the following morning we were back at the yard and watching the daughter do a few jumps on him. Without reservation, I knew he was the one for me, so after inspection of all the documents, including the vetting they had undertaken only six months earlier, we agreed on the sale. My heart was full to overflowing, it was such a joy to be in a positive place again with an amazing adventure to look forward to.

It was time to go home so my sister and husband drove with us as far as Truro to show us the quickest route back and we all had one final stop at a local shopping village. In the middle of all the shops there was a large equestrian centre and the reality of what was happening began to hit. I was stroking the saddle pads and horse rugs with my own horse in mind, this was really going to happen. I bought a schooling crop and it is one of my most treasured possessions, whenever I pick it up, it always takes me right back to that moment, stood in a shop in Truro, bursting with happiness.

As soon as I returned I arranged for a vetting the following Friday and a horse transporter who had availability to bring him to Cheshire the following Monday. Vetting was fine, although with a strange twist of irony Pudding does suffer from slight hay fever and has to wear a nose net on really bad days. Other than that, it

Maybe it was just me doing all the drinking..

was fine. I spoke with the vet on the phone and he did comment on how calm Pudding was

"You've got a good one there"

I felt sure I had.

I am thankful that I bought from such lovely people as they could easily have cancelled the sale on the morning of his transport to Cheshire and here's why. Having taken a note of their bank details I sent a pound through using my online banking to check all was fine and had immediate confirmation that it had been received. I then sent the much larger final balance through. Both parties waited patiently but nothing arrived. We spoke on the phone and decided that it may be a bank system that needed to refresh overnight, so the money would obviously be there in the morning. Morning arrived and still nothing – it was still marked as pending on my account. I contacted the bank who said it was being reviewed by the fraud team and could not specify when the funds would be released. I phoned and desperately hoped they would be understanding and thankfully they were, taking a leap of faith they released the horse with only a scanned copy of my driving licence and a utility bill as any real security. It must have been truly nerve racking for them, as the money did not get to them for another two days. Thank goodness for people who are prepared to trust.

The big day arrived, and I got the text at eight thirty to say my special delivery was on its way. This had been a torturous week, I couldn't sleep for excitement and simply could not wait for him to get here. The stable had fresh shavings, the haynet was up and the water bucket was full. I got a text from the driver saying was ten minutes away just as he was turning into the drive, he had made record time and I seriously wondered exactly how fast he must have been driving to make it from Cornwall in just over four and half hours. We opened the side door to see a pretty stressed Pudding. The floor was covered in poo and he was snorting wildly. While the driver took himself off for a toilet break I brought Pudding off the van and walked him round to his stable. I'm not sure what I was expecting our first moments together would be like, but they were pretty unremarkable. He had the most enormous wee, walked around the stable a few times sniffing the air, then stood there looking absolutely shattered. He hardly had time to catch his breath when the livery owner arrived and stuck the worming solution down his mouth

"He will need to stay in tomorrow while the solution works its way through" she said "then we can put him in the field".

After a few moments of friendly small talk, she disappeared and left me alone with Pudding. He stood there with his eyes half open and my heart went out to him, he'd just had one hell of a morning. I got my grooming kit out and gently brushed him until his bottom lip dropped and his eyes seemed virtually closed, then quietly left the stable so he could get some rest.

The horse I left was tired and placid, nothing like the agitated horse which greeted me the following morning. This was the first time I had been next to him when his head was fully in the air and towering over mine, he now seemed enormous. Quite frankly, he scared the life out of me. Whilst I had felt comfortable riding the nice horses at the riding school, I simply didn't have any familiarity with how horses behave. He moved constantly, being stuck in a small confined space with an agitated horse when you don't know if they are going to kick out or bite is a terrifying experience. He had no real acknowledgement of me and was happy to push past me to crane his head over the stable door. He would leap into action whenever he heard the sound of another horse and whinny loudly. He could just about get his head over the back wall to see the horses in the stables behind him and I found I had to get out of the way pretty quickly if he suddenly decided to change his viewing position from the stable door to the over the back wall.

Determined to get a grip on things I decided to take him for a walk around the yard, so he could orientate himself a little better. With trembling hands, I put the head collar on, opened the stable door and off we went. He was completely preoccupied with his surrounds and paying absolutely no attention to me whatsoever. I walked him into the ménage, as it seemed the most sensible thing to do, if he did decide to make a run for it then he couldn't go far. He snorted the entire time we walked and lent over the ménage wall to view the horses in the surrounding fields while letting out a series of head-held-high-full-pitched-whinnies. The response was immediate; five horses came galloping across the field to see who the new boy was. I was rapidly learning that the sound of galloping horses will put most horses on high alert, at best – if not send them into a frantic gallop themselves. This is a sound that signals a lion is lurking somewhere and if you don't run then you are going to be someone's dinner.

He did a little jump on the spot, head in the air snorting and his whole body tensed and shook, ready for a quick escape if necessary. If he wasn't convinced there was something frightening before, then one look at me would have confirmed it. I felt like the one with a wild tiger, which I was now holding by the tail. No amount of walk trot transitions had prepared me for this - what the hell do I do now? I stood rooted to the spot, unable to either move or breathe. My head was racing, I was terrified. I even contemplated just letting go of the lead rope and running for help. Somewhere in my head I could hear my dad's voice 'come on Cazzy, you can do it'. He had never run from anything in his life, so I found my one remaining atom of guts and decided to man up. With one deft jerk I pulled Pudding round and marched him back to the stable.

This is new for both of us

Once back in the stable I felt we needed somehow to get acquainted. I have always been a 'feeder' so it made total sense to me that I should get my bag of carrots and give him a little treat, and indeed, the treat was very well received. What wasn't so well received was the nip I got a few minutes later when he felt I wasn't forthcoming enough with more carrots. In fact, I spent the next hour trying to keep my hands as far away from this horse's mouth as possible, as any line of sight he had to my fingers prompted a lunge forward in the hope of goodies. At this point I had completely forgotten the 'dream' and felt like I was suddenly propelled into a 'nightmare'.

Where was my lovely, quiet horse, and what in god's name was I landed with instead?

That night I hardly got a wink of sleep. I lay awake, terrified of facing him the following morning. Usually nothing will put me off my breakfast, but I couldn't eat a thing. As I drove to the yard I began to feel I had made a terrible mistake and things didn't improve when I got there. He had now been in his stable for two days and nights and for a horse which usually lives out, that was more than he could handle. He was in a foul mood and very restless. I begged the livery yard owner to get him out in the field as quickly as possible.

"No problem, you go and get him and bring him around now," she said.

I began to panic at the prospect of doing this, I had hoped she would volunteer to do it for me. Head collar on we ventured forth, he was snorting, his head towering over mine and dancing around like Fred Astaire. My heart was racing so quickly I thought it was likely to jump out of my chest, I had literally no idea what he was going to do next. Possibly bolt, rear up, who knows? We were clearly a million miles away from the horse I thought I'd bought. We crossed the lane leading to his paddock and I was told to wait and let Pudding and the horse he was soon to be sharing a field with sniff each other under the fence while she deposited her horse in another field. I stood there like a human statue while they sniffed and squealed. I was very firm on her return.

"You're taking him in the field," I said.

She marched him, unhooked the lead rope and off he went in full gallop. After several circuits of the field, he eventually slowed down and made a more formal greeting to his new field mate. Then off again when he realised there was a field full of mares next door eager to see who the feisty new blood was. He did a full fly past, head held high, tail held high and on full-high kicking trot – it was almost comical, like the donkey from Shrek in parade mode.

Eventually he calmed down, had a roll and settled into munching his way through the plentiful grass. I stayed for a while watching him, went back and mucked out, then returned again to find the scene little changed from when I left it.

In the car going home I pondered on what had happened and felt a strong wave of terror at the prospect of ever getting him out of the field. I had made a decision that no matter what it took, I would bring him in every day for the first week to groom him and give him a little feed. I had to create routine and develop some discipline, or it was sorely tempting just to leave him there and spare myself the emotional rollercoaster.

And so that is what I did. I rose every morning and was at the field by 8 a.m., bringing him in then turning him back out. I lost half a stone in the first week as my stomach was literally too churned up to eat. Every day he seemed calmer and more settled and by the end of the first week he seemed so much more like the horse I had viewed. The terrors of walking into a field of horses who towered over me certainly wasn't dissipating. Nor was the battle between man and beast when it came to bringing him in. When he dug his heels in and refused to budge, there was literally no moving him. On the first morning this happened I decided to go and get help. One of the older and wiser liveries came to the paddock with me and she began to push him to one side until he eventually conceded and walked on.

The next morning, I had a terrifying game of catch me. As soon as I approached he galloped off, I followed him down to the bottom of the field and got him in a corner when he turned and galloped past me, only a few feet away from where I was standing. There was a huge part of me just wanted to turn around, walk out of the field and never go back. But then the other, more belligerent side came into play. The little bugger was not going to beat me, so if it took all day he was coming out of that field with me. What I now know is that Pudding rarely has either the stomach or the energy to fight for too long, so after a few more attempts and with my heart in my mouth, he stood still long enough for me to get hold of him and lead him out. I had managed to get hold of a Monty Roberts head collar which proved to be the best purchase ever. My secret weapon here was nose pressure. I stuck this head collar on him and whenever we walked forward and then stopped and refused to move, I would pull on the pressure point, only releasing it the second he started walking again. In no time at all he stopped fighting.

I have not really mentioned my husband Phil yet, so now seems a good time to do so. We have been married for a lifetime, have three grown daughters and I love him to bits. He always has something to say, has a great sense of humour and will want to get involved in anything new. He couldn't wait to see Pudding on the night he arrived and was greeted by the horse he remembered, calm, placid and quite frankly shattered after the long journey from Cornwall. The following evening on the way to the yard we stopped off at a local equine supplier to get some bits.

"I'm going to buy him some treats," my husband said.
"Oh, don't do that," I said, "horses are not like dogs, they can bite...please don't."

Too late. My husband, buoyed on by the previous encounters with the dog who would instantly be his best friend on the production of treats, stood at the counter making the purchase. He bounced into the livery yard like a superhero who has just found his powers and stood in front of the stable door dishing out treats to Pudding at quite a rate. Now if you have ever wondered how far a horse's neck can stretch, let me tell you, it is quite a way. As Pudding practiced his extending neck routine, he now had Phil pinned against the wall and I watched my husband get mugged. Pudding had the packet and the last laugh. It was some time before Phil agreed to come down to the yard with me again; as a city boy not used to animals, being shook down by a half-tonne animal took a few weeks to get over.

Now we were getting on for nearly two weeks and I still had not got the nerve to ride him. I was generally feeling a lot calmer about being around Pudding and good doses of Coldplay's 'Hymn for the Weekend' on the way to the livery yard certainly helped to put in me in a positive frame of mind. Ria called in to see how I was doing and when I explained the situation she had the perfect solution which came in the shape of a young instructor called Amy. We set off to visit the neighbouring yard where she worked, and she smiled when I explained that I needed someone to help me ride him for the first time, as I had completely lost my bottle. Sure enough, three days later, there we all were. Amy was a fearless eventer and her stunned face when I brought this small, hairy pony into the ménage was an absolute picture. Her face said it all .....'Really?'

I took a deep breath and climbed on-board. Suddenly I felt exactly the same way I did back on the moors. Safe. We trotted round, with Amy providing some brief direction and the whole thing ended on a high.

The following day my sister came to visit, so Pudding and I did some manoeuvres while she recorded me on her phone. I was feeling more relaxed, as was Pudding; so much so that by fourth day of riding it was a struggle to get him moving at any pace at all. He had already figured out that I was not going to push him, so he relaxed with the very firm attitude – if you want it, then you are going to have to make me. I was still unbalanced and producing a wide range of very dodgy signals and there were points when not even I was sure what I was asking him to do. Not many horses would have put up with me but thankfully, this little chap was quite happy to potter along with me until I got my act together.

My two special boys

Sometime later one of the liveries, a man called Jonny who had several horses which he produced and sold, recounted something from those early days. He was on the other side of the ménage with a vet who was conducting a vetting on one of his horses when they found themselves just watching me. The vet looked at Jonny and said 'That's some cob.'

Now the yard I am based at is much bigger than the average. Nestled in the Cheshire countryside, there are around forty horses based there, with a big American style barn at the heart of things. People are friendly, love their horses and there is a huge mix of ages and abilities. I found myself quickly drawn to two ladies who were the founding members of The Cob Club, a rather tongue in cheek name given by the yard owner for all the middle-aged ladies who have hairy cobs they just hack out on. Both were genuine, fun, unassuming, and above all, very welcoming. Janet is tall, quiet, always with a pleasant word, yet a little nervous about riding, which is totally at odds with her ability. In all the time I have now known her, she's seen me fall off three times and I have never seen her anywhere but firmly in the saddle. Ruth always looks like she just got out of bed, but a warmer hearted person you couldn't find. She would literally do anything for anyone. It was Ruth who made the first invitation.

"Come and join us for a hack on Sunday. We're not adventurous," she said, "it takes us a moment to decide whether to trot or not, but you are very welcome to come."

All Sunday the only thing I could think about was the hack at 2 p.m. I got to the yard at midday, grabbed Pudding from the field, groomed him and was tacked up and ready to go. I was the only one wearing a body protector and my huge one at that. Once I put my high vis over the top I looked like an enormous barrel, the same width as the blessed horse. I was aware I looked ridiculous, but I had no intention of being a YouTube clip or spending any time in hospital, I was taking no chances!

It was a beautiful sunny afternoon as the three of us proceeded down the main driveway and out of the front gates. At this point it is worth noting that these ladies may play down their abilities, but they will hack where even hardened eventers might fear to tread. The road on which the livery yard is based stretches for a good mile in either direction and whilst it should be a quiet country lane, it has in fact become a rat run for motorists wishing to bypass the town centre. As we made our way along we were overtaken by a steady stream of cars: tankers, tractors, cyclists, motorbikes, in fact just about any mode of transport you can think of, some so close I could have reached through the open passenger window and changed the radio channel. Neither lady batted an eyelid. Thankfully, neither did Pudding. He plodded behind taking it all in stride for which I will be eternally grateful.

We came to a bend in the road where a road sign had fallen over, and both the mares planted their feet and refused to budge. The cars started to build up behind us and I was expecting some more of the abuse I had experienced earlier in the ride from drivers who clearly felt that horses should not be on any part of the route they had chosen to travel.

"Do you think Pudding will go past?" shouted Ruth. I gave Pudding a nudge and my heart filled with pride as he casually walked past the stationary mares and the road sign and continued to lead our happy little bunch until we got to the bridle path.

Once on the bridle path, the challenges kept coming thick and fast. Families with children screaming and running around; dogs running up and barking; horses, goats and chickens just beyond the hedge and a small stretch where they were constructing new houses – so all the things which can easily send horses in to a frenzy, like stacks of pipes, cranes and things wrapped in loose plastic which blow in the breeze. I was now feeling that someone must have been looking after me when I bought this horse, as he went past everything without even blinking.

We reached a point on the track where the ladies normally take the opportunity to use the neighbouring field for a canter.

"Would you like a canter?" chirped Ruth
'No" was my firm reply.

I had built up the bottle to tackle todays ride and was enjoying it, but that was a step more than my nerves could handle. It would be a good few weeks before I was prepared to canter Pudding anywhere.

By the time we eventually made it back to the yard there was simply nothing else I could think of that would normally spook a horse that we hadn't actually encountered today. I dismounted and spent five minutes telling Pudding how good he was, stroking and patting him like a lunatic while he stood there looking somewhat bemused. The truth is that I was so profoundly relieved that he had been so good and not done anything stupid. He got double treats before being returned to the field.

I guess, like any addiction, you begin with the small amount and then before you know it, it has taken over. This was certainly the case with this little horse. I was so thrilled at the fact he was a darling to ride when we were out, I felt driven to want to ride him more and more. Not yet at the stage where I felt remotely comfortable with the idea of going out on my own, I would set myself some practice time every couple of days.

I know myself well enough to understand that when I am trying to learn something, I prefer to go off by myself and give it a go until I get some sort of handle on it. When I was younger and had parts to learn for amateur dramatics, I would disappear into my bedroom to learn my lines and then spent hours walking around the garden reciting them to myself. When I was at college I decided to progress from my bicycle to a little motorbike, a very utilitarian Honda 90 with panniers and a front box for all my books. On evening of its arrival, I took myself off to a set of quiet little side streets and just practiced, until I had worked out how the manoeuvre the bike, change the gears and brake. Once I have the basics I just like to get on with it.

The yard had clear peak flow times, it was incredibly busy first thing in the morning when everyone arrived to sort things out before going to work and again at three when schools finished through to early evening when everyone returned from work. Those who weren't working would show up to ride just after nine in the morning and leave by midday when they had completed all their jobs. That left a magical window between one and two thirty when the yard was almost empty. I know you should never ride when there is no one around for safety reasons, but somewhere pottering around was the yard owner, doing some little job or other. So, I could ride without anyone interfering, commenting, watching or interrupting. I would arrive, get the tack balanced on the stable door and walk over to get Pudding from his paddock. During the winter months when the grass had stopped growing, he had no objections to coming in a little earlier, it meant he had access to food slightly sooner than he thought he would. I could definitely sense a slump as we turned into his aisle, walked towards the stable and he spotted the tack, this meant work not food.

Once in the ménage I would practice trotting; straight lines, circles, diagonals, you name it. And when I felt relaxed enough I would try for a little canter. Little being the operative word, after about four strides Pudding would drop down a gear and we would be back to trot. To be honest, I was generally quite happy with this arrangement.

There was one afternoon though when I had set my heart on cantering. I put my body protector on and was determined that we were not leaving until we had done at least one circuit of the ménage. I can imagine that my riding confused Pudding endlessly; whenever I wanted him to go faster I would do the exact opposite of what you are supposed to do. I would sit forward and my hands would rock as though I was rowing a boat. For nearly thirty minutes we laboured on, trotting then a few steps of canter, then trotting again, then eureka it happened – I sat back, grabbed the saddle strap and Pudding went for it. Round and round we cantered, looking back it really wasn't that fast, but it felt as though we were flying at the time. There was no steering on my part, I was just getting to grips with the whole feeling and it was an absolute adrenaline rush.

For the next few weeks I would enjoy my very own little sessions with Pudding, getting my head around with some of the basics. I began to understand how it would feel and after many attempts, felt that I could let go of the saddle strap and try a little steering. We always did enormous loops of the double ménage, but I was quite happy with that. You have to start somewhere right?

Sadly, any school holidays would put a pin in my balloon, as most of the teenagers spent the day at the yard and there was always one or two of them cantering in circles or jumping a metre.

Chapter Four

Years before, I had often seen vans and lorries carrying horses at all hours of the day and thought it must be an absolute chore to have your weekends continually disturbed by horse commitments. I fully understand it now, it's an absolute drug, you get addicted and want more and more. After the first hack, I sought every opportunity to get out and about. Our yard has its own private Facebook page and any livery can post messages, I always the first to respond to any message asking if anyone wanted to go out for a ride.

On one particular trip there was some debate about who would go, as there was a new horse on the yard. He was a trotter, and the new owner was trying to teach him to canter properly. It was agreed that only those willing to canter would go, and although my heart was racing, I dug deep in the drawer for my brave-pants and was going to give it a go. It is worth knowing that the bridle path we use is actually completely unsuitable for horses going any faster than a walk. It is very narrow and has quite a few blind corners, often with dog walkers taking a cheeky pootle on the horse track; but the real concern are the trees whose trunks and branches have formed a trajectory running straight across the path at head level. If you don't remember to duck, then you will find yourself hanging out of a tree, or worse still, without a head.

As we arrived at the chosen spot, the two younger horses set off and then Pudding took the signal and off we went. I promise you, this was no gentle canter – in a bid to catch the horses in front he went into full gallop, my reins were everywhere. I was desperately trying to duck to avoid the trees and every time I leaned forward to avoid decapitation, Pudding took it as a signal to pick up speed. We rounded the final bend to see the two lead horses waiting by the gate. Pudding applied full brakes and we narrowly avoided a crash.

"Are you alright? they asked

In truth, I really was. My head was telling me that I should be traumatised, yet when I checked, I found I was fine. The adrenaline was pumping, at no time did I actually feel as though I was going to fall off, I was buzzing from head to toe. That said, if they had wanted to go back and do it again, I would probably have said no.

Once we got back at the yard I reflected that I had no idea Pudding could move so quickly. The Mighty Midget could pack quite a punch when he put his mind to it, which thankfully was not that often.

It was now several weeks into owning Pudding and he was becoming the horse that I hoped he would be. After the first high octane week he had settled down and seemed to be enjoying life. The yard was filled with lots of pleasant people and I loved getting out and about with Ruth and Janet, we would potter along and generally chat about all the things middle aged women talk about; men, children, dogs and food. Horses featured quite heavily in most chats, with the usual debate about what and when to feed them, when to rug them and the individual traits of each horse. Thus far I had experienced quite an easy time of it, the horses were still out on summer livery which simply meant they lived in the field.

The amount of work required in looking after them was minimal. Ria was astounded when I said I only went down to see him once a day

"Once a day! Doesn't he come in at night?"

"Nope"

"What about giving him his breakfast and tea?"

"He doesn't have any"

"That's just too easy. I can't believe you only go down once a day"

"Well how many times do I need to check he's still in the field?" I replied.

The switch to winter livery in November came as I complete shock to the system. I was on a 'Do It Yourself' arrangement as it was simply the cheapest way to keep a horse. And believe me, there is *nothing* cheap about keeping a horse. However much you think it's going to cost, double it. I had decided to give myself some time off from working, after decades of hard endeavour it was lovely to take a break and live a little. I had received quite a sizeable amount of redundancy of which a set amount was allotted as 'horse money'. I quickly learned that there is a whole range of kit and accessories you need to look after your horse; forks, buckets, brushes, shovels, poo pickers, wheelbarrows, food bins, bedding, haynets; the list goes on and on. My eyes were opened to the billion-pound industry that is equine supplies. Along with all the essentials, come the desirables. Rugs for your horse; winter ones, summer ones; fly rugs, lightweight, medium weight, heavy weight, under-blankets, stable blankets – you get the picture. And with each season comes the latest colours and fashions, as hard as it is to imagine there are colours trending right now in equestrian circles. If you really want to turn on the style then you will go 'matchy, matchy' and present your horse in co-ordinated saddlecloths, ear covers, leg wraps and you too will be sporting a riding jacket in the same colour. Obviously, this seasons colour. I found a clearance website selling quality gear from last season's stock and bought all my essentials from there.

Walking through the door of my local equine supplier was like Alice falling into Horse Wonderland, floor to rafters filled with every conceivable horse related product. Walls full of horse supplements; things to calm them down, give them energy, for hooves, shiny coats, muscle development, veterans you name it. More shampoos than my local pharmacist. The heady aroma of leather; saddles, bridles, riding boots, riding jackets. Walls full of hats; velvet ones, sparkly ones, those for serious eventers. Saddle cloths, numnahs, leg wraps, ear covers and my personal weakness – rugs. For a small hairy horse who needs no covers at all, I actually have more rugs than is possibly imaginable. He is never knowingly under-rugged.

This was the saddlery from which I purchased my riding hat and a few months later my boots. I had been telling Phil that I needed a proper grip on my ankles to ride properly, so he offered to get me a pair of boots. For the second time we were greeted by the manager, who was delighted to see Phil and more than happy to spend as much time as necessary to ensure I got a 'good pair of boots'. He sat on the sofa for nearly an hour while I tried on one pair after another, until the manager declared that the pair I was wearing were the right ones for me. They did feel like they gripped my leg firmly and looked quite robust. Apparently, they are Ariat, which she felt would immediately make us coo with delight, but instead she was greeted with blank faces. We were just beginning to get to grips with Equine Branding. Although Phil was pretty sure they must be endorsed by Royalty or something of that nature when we found ourselves stood at the till point for the second time, with our mouths wide open, about to part with nearly three hundred pounds.

"That bloody woman" he muttered as we left.

I often walk through the clothing section and paw the gorgeous selection of garments. I once made the mistake of asking the assistant which would be the best little white top to use under my black jacket for a dressage test. She took me to a rather fetching little Pikeur number which she politely handed to me

"this one is lovely" she said looking admiringly at it.

Indeed it was, I held it in my hands and my eye caught the price tag, it was nearly two hundred pounds. Dear God, you have got to be kidding me.

"Do people actually pay that much for these tops?"

She looked shocked and stared directly into my eyes "yes madam. It's *Pikeur*"

What I had seen as I wandered around was a gorgeous high brand all weather top in emerald green, which is one of my favourite colours. I didn't buy it there and then, but it festered in the back of my mind until in the end I could stand it no longer and went and bought the thing, and the jodhpurs to match. The following weekend regaled in my new outfit I went out on my hack feeling a million dollars and I am convinced that my riding improved exponentially just by wearing it. It was one of our round the world hacks which took nearly all day, but I did not mind in the least, as we passed cars or windows I could see my reflection. Oh yes, this was very pleasing indeed. On our return we spent a few minutes chatting as usual, it was then I noticed that there was a huge amount of bobbling under my arms. And on closer inspection around my chest as well. Horrified I showed Janet

"Look at this, can you believe it" I exclaimed
"You've got boob bobbling" she laughed "It looks like you've got twenty nipples"

Outraged I put on another top and headed straight for the store, where the assistant quietly examined the item. Without a word she signalled for another assistant to come over and they both looked at. The second assistant then picked up the special phone, the one behind the till point which I had never seen used. She spoke in muffled tones, but I could just about make out 'yes, yes, immediately' returned to me and with sombre tones informed me that she had spoken to the manufacturer and she was to give me a full refund and destroy the top immediately. They had noted the batch number and all remaining tops in that batch could also be destroyed. It was all about brand reputation.
"Ariat do not bobble".

Back to winter livery and a week in and I was beginning to see what Ria meant, horse commitments take over everything. I had to be at the stables first thing in the morning to take Pudding over to the field. Then came the chores; mucking out, filling the haynets and making sure the water buckets were clean and re-filled. At two in the afternoon I would drive back and collect him from the field and deposit him back in his stable. It was hard work, I found I was living in my jodhpurs as there seemed hardly any point in changing when I got home, so generally I looked permanently scruffy and smelt of horse pee.

I had made the decision to bring him in between two and three in the afternoon after the disastrous first night. We had all received a text from the livery owner saying that she was bringing forward the winter livery date and from that Saturday all horses needed to be brought out of the field to over-night in their stable. I had already arranged to be out on Saturday as Phil and I were going to drive to the Peak District to catch up with his sister and join in her lunchtime birthday celebrations. At that point I had no concerns, as I felt that we would comfortably be back for five o'clock when most of the other liveries had said they would bring their horses over. The afternoon did not go as I had planned, the meal was delayed, everyone was having a good time and Phil was keen to hold on until some of the other relatives arrived, so he could say hello. By five thirty my stress levels were through the roof, with a tight ball of tension in my stomach I had lost the power to small talk with anyone, as all I could think about was the fact it was going dark and Pudding was out there on his own. I congratulate myself that I did not in fact explode, as I really felt like doing, but managed to get Phil to say his goodbyes and get going. By the time we got to the yard it was gone seven and pitch black.

There are many things I like about the yard, but the fact that Pudding is in a field on the other side of the busy road is not one of them. Furthermore, he cannot see any horses or even lights from where he is, and you have to get him through two gates and negotiate a ten-minute walk down the road before you get to the main gates into the yard. There are no street lights, no pavement and motorists are literally upon you before they have any idea you are there. To add to this already potent mix comes the fact that horses are herd animals and go frantic when they are left on their own. Especially if they have seen all the other horses leave the field and they are still stuck there. Trying to lead any horse who has got himself into a state is a frightening proposition, they are erratic, spooked out by everything and likely to spin, rear or drag you along.

I stood by the stable quickly trying to decide what was the best thing to do. I had my high vis on and Phil had the torch. A month before I had bought a fluorescent band with red flashing lights from Aldi, it was in the cyclists' section, but it seemed like something that would work really well on my riding hat. The lights could be switched on and they emitted a red flash which was really quite bright on a winters day. It seemed like a good idea to put my riding hat on with the fluorescent band, I figured Pudding would need to know where I was, as would motorists.

"I'll go into the field and shine the torch" said Phil "and you call him"

We ran along the road and over to the field, there was not one jot of light anywhere, Phil had to keep the torch in front of us both, so we could at least see where we were going. We opened the gate to the paddock and went in. There was no sign of him anywhere.

"Pudding, Pudding, come here boy" I shouted while Phil flashed the torch around the field.

Suddenly in the distance we saw a slight movement as Pudding came into view. He was nervous and wired, he looked ready to bolt at a moment's notice.

"Phil, he's petrified. Stop waving the torch around you're frightening him"
"I'm frightening him! What about the alien invasion on the top of your head?"

Ignoring him I continued shouting "Pudding, come on now"

He slowly and nervously worked his way towards me until I was close enough to get hold of him and whizz the head collar on. He pushed his way towards the gate and spun out of it, swinging directly round to face me. The light from the torch was swinging wildly back and forth as Phil tried to find his way out of the field and provide me with some light at the same time, every time the beam moved away the dim red flash of my headgear seemed to light up Puddings eyes and looked like something out of horsemen of the apocalypse.

Somehow, we all made it through the second gate and at some pace down the road, through the main gate onto the yard. Once he was in his stable we felt we could finally breathe. That was the point when I vowed I would never be the last one to bring my horse in. Ever.

It was a week or two later when I realised that some time ago I had bought tickets for a Monty Roberts demonstration and the event was actually that Saturday. I let Phil know 'You're going to see Monty Roberts on Saturday'. He was a little disappointed as we stood in the queue to enter and he discovered it wasn't The Don of gardening we were waiting to see.

This Monty was a legend of the horse world. From America, he had trained champions time and time again, but more than that, he seemed to understand what made horses tick. He was a real, live Horse Whisperer, and we had front row seats. As we sat waiting for things to begin, we were informed the event was being filmed by Horse and Country.

Just as the show started Kelly Marks looked out over the crowd, announcing 'Now usually there is a bored husband who has been dragged here by his wife, sitting with his arms crossed and in direct camera line to anything we are doing'.

With Monty Roberts

I looked at Phil and he dutifully uncrossed his arms. When things got going, even Phil sat forward in his seat soaking it all in. We saw one horse after another enter the round-pen with a problem and leave without it. But there was the equine magic trick that occurred before any intercession, something called 'Join Up'. It is a simple process, which if followed correctly, allows the horse to select you as its leader. It transpired that the most important thing you can do for a horse, is to generate their respect; all the love and gushy stuff comes after that. If you don't gain their respect, then they will push you around and generally do what they like. It seemed like a no-brainer that gaining this respect was obviously what you want to aim for.

Fired up by the demonstration, I determined that I was going to do Join Up first thing on Monday morning, even though Monday arrived and it was absolutely chucking it down. I made a rudimentary round-pen using jump wings, poles and incorporating the side of the ménage fence. As there were not enough poles and jump wings to make a decent sized pen, it was by any measure a pretty small space, but it was more or less round and it would just have to do.

I led Pudding in and he wandered over to the fence to stare at the mares, completely ignoring me. Taking the deepest breath, I began - snapping the lead rope in front of me, I stared into his eyes and made an aggressive step towards him. Pudding galvanised into action and started cantering around the makeshift pen only feet away from me. I kept the pressure on – one, two, three, four, five, six times around in the same direction. Not moving my eyes from his, I made a step towards him as though to block his path and he quickly turned and cantered in the opposite direction. And again, six times round the pen. One last time I stepped out and he moved to go the other way – this time I was looking for signs that he was submitting. Anything, licking of the lips – nope. Head lowering – yes, his head was definitely hanging lower in a submissive manner. OK then, here goes, I stopped the pressure, dropped my eyes and head and turned my back to him. I could sense that he had stopped and a moment later was standing directly behind me. I walked away and he followed. I changed direction and he came with me. It was done, I turned, stroked him and he nuzzled me. Whilst I cannot quite put my finger on what exactly changed, something did. There was a connection that happened that day that just ended up getting stronger and stronger. I would love to say he listened to my every word from that point and was never a prat again, but that wouldn't be true. But he watches me, he watches to see how I react to things and I see a change in the decisions he makes based on my reactions.

This was something that was brought home to me so clearly one evening. I had arrived to bring Pudding in and found myself in a somewhat jittery mood. That morning I had walked Pudding into his paddock as usual and left the gate open, which I had done many times before without incident, but today he back-tracked and charged down the path to eat the lush grass that grew on the path edge. I understood why, there was simply no grass left in his paddock and he is the ultimate opportunist. The front gate was shut, so he couldn't get onto the road, but he was defiantly not letting me anywhere near him. As I approached, he would speed off. When we eventually worked our way to the other end of the path and a locked gate, he turned and galloped past me. I still find being anywhere near a half-tonne horse when it's in full charge very unnerving, to say the least. I had to go and get help to round him up and deposit him in his paddock – so when the evening came I was already feeling quite highly strung and wanting to put myself back in control.

As I entered his paddock, he stood waiting for me and I put on his head collar and began the walk back through the mud. He managed to get a better pace than me and pulled ever so slightly ahead, but this was enough. Without any real justification, I yanked the lead rope and told him off for barging. He looked at me; my rapid breath, shaky voice and racing heart and decided there must be BIG trouble somewhere. Within seconds, his breath was racing, he had his head held high, trying to swing round and jumping on the spot.

"Go and get Fleur," I shouted to my young stable neighbour.

Naomi ran off and within minutes Fleur appeared. Now this is a woman who was born on a horse. She owns several enormous ex-racehorses who she works wonders with. I held her in the highest esteem the minute I discovered she rode the churlish, temperamental 18 hands high mare who you quite literally can't see over the back of. Anyone who can do that knows a thing or two in my book. Fleur took charge of the situation immediately.

"Don't look at him, look forward and walk in a firm but steady manner out of the gate." We set off down the road, my heart still beating wildly. Fleur walked alongside me talking to me through every step.

"Don't talk to him, keep your eyes ahead of you, come on you're doing really well."

We marched along, Pudding puffing and snorting alongside me, but thankfully now walking at a steady pace, while I had my eyes fixed firmly on the gate to the yard. Once we were through, I relaxed a little but kept going until all three of us had marched him into the stable. Once Fleur and Naomi had gone, I slid down the stable door and slumped to the floor. 'What the hell..' Why on earth was I frightening myself half to death like this?
It made perfect sense to go home, have a nice cup of tea and think about it when I had calmed down.

Since that time, I have often reflected on these moments and have come to understand an old saying that a horse is a reflection of their owner. It is miraculous that they can sense the slightest change in your breath, heart rate, eye movement or body posture. They know when you are scared or relaxed and will take their cue from you. In all the years of corporate training, all the text books and managers meetings – nothing has taught me to think about how I respond to things in the way that little horse has.

Naomi's two horses occupied the stables next to mine. She was a typical teenager in many senses – absolutely no fear whatsoever. Her mother Delores was bottle blonde, with long, painted nails and as is the custom with apple-shaped women, she loved to wear black leggings and a capacious top. I liked her, but she came with a health warning – once you start talking to her that was it for the evening. Even if you had to break the conversation to go and get hay/feed/stable rug/anything she would follow you there and back talking the entire time. And every sentence began with "I'm not being funny but..."

"I'm not being funny, but that fence has been broken for months and it doesn't matter how many times I tell her, she doesn't bother to go and fix it. I'm not being funny, but the quality of this hay is ridiculous. We pay a lot for this livery and we shouldn't be given sub-standard hay like this."

The topics rarely varied, she was unhappy with virtually everything and seemed sure that if she listed all the failings often enough, then you too would be as unhappy as she was. She was standing by our paddock gate with Naomi the evening

I had my meltdown. When Naomi suggested that she could bring Pudding in, Delores was quick to interject

"I'm not being funny, but it's not your horse Naomi and you're not covered on insurance if you have an accident and..."

"I don't want her to bring him in," I cut across, "I need to win this battle."

I liked Naomi. She was pleasant teenager, a fastidious bordering on OCD stable cleaner, and she loved her horses. As an only child she had managed to wrap her parents around her little finger, they were simply powerless to resist her requests and I am not sure she had ever heard the word No. This, in part, was the reason she had two horses. One had a poorly back and couldn't be ridden for a few months, so she decided she simply couldn't be without a horse for that long, spotted a mare Jonny was selling and within a couple of days it belonged to her. I couldn't even begin to imagine how much it was costing in livery bills.

The following Sunday morning Naomi asked if she could join our hack and we agreed. There was a little concern behind the scenes that we may be considered as having responsibility for her, none of us could imagine what a rainstorm of crap the parents would bring down on us if anything happened to their darling daughter. However, off we went all the same.

The hack began as they had always done, Pudding and I went last as he was the slowest and we plodded along enjoying the sunshine and scenery. Before long, we had snaked our way through the lanes to a second livery yard and collected an attractive blonde on a nervous mare and she soon took charge.

"Now we have to cross a busy road and hack down it for about fifty yards, so I need you all together and no stragglers. Are you ready? Go..."

Our now considerable body of horses all set off together at quite the pace, Pudding even broke out into canter to try and keep up. Such was the clatter of hooves, motorists slowed down to see what the commotion was and children on back seats waved merrily. As soon as we turned off the main road, we were quickly down a little lane, past a country pub and some quaint cottages before stopping at The Lines. This is a long stretch of disused railway line up at tree top level, which has to be accessed by a 1:2 gradient set of steps. Blondie directed operations and we all felt immediately relieved that she had. We were given our place in the line and we steadily climbed to the top. Once there, the track ran as far as the eye could see in either direction, flanked by tree tops and bushes, there were occasional breaks in the foliage where you could look down on the rolling fields or meandering streams. It was simply magical.

After a short spell in walk, Blondie announced we should have a trot. We gathered our reins and off we all went. I had noticed that Pudding was becoming lighter in his step and really picking up pace, he had nudged past the other horses and was now firmly placed in second position behind Blondie and her highly strung mare. Even when we stopped, he was agitated, restless and refused to stand still, it felt like someone had given him a double red bull. There was something about one of the mares that seemed to be firing him up. He had always taken a great interest in The Ladies, but he had two new feisty mares today and he was fresh as they come.

"Be firm with him" encouraged Blondie "make him stand still"
"I'm trying" I replied weakly

I was used to him doing what I asked, and I had no real idea how to get him to stand still. I pulled the reins and he reversed then moved off again. So we just ended up doing circles; circles that took us off in an opposite direction to the group, then even more circles to get us moving back towards them again.

We had a hip flask full of port and brandy, a family pack of topic bars and a few now crushed packets of cheesy biscuits and we were determined to make the most of them. Obviously, I only had the opportunity to enjoy things when my current circle was close enough for me to reach whatever was being passed around. There was a small panic as Ruth leaned over to take a photograph and her saddle flipped round sending her hurtling to the ground. She was clearly shaken and sore, but this woman is hard-core. She laughed it off and we all commenced in search for something she could use as a mounting block, so she could get back on her horse. We found a ménage nestled behind a wall and shamelessly broke in, got Ruth mounted and made a hasty retreat.

Back on the lines, Pudding started to become harder to handle. Naomi's mare Spotty had broken away from the group and Naomi was really struggling to keep her under control. She was putting in one rear after another and was steadily moving further and further away from us. Pudding seemed to be locked into her every move. As Spotty began to break away, I couldn't keep him still and I made the stupid mistake of following her. We headed off down the track watching Naomi and Spotty move into the distance and worryingly we were getting faster and faster in pursuit, it occurred to me that we may just end up bolting at this rate. My second mistake was shortening the reins to try and pull Pudding to a stop. I now know horses ride into pressure and today was no exception, we really were going at quite a pace.

As we got closer and closer to the steps I saw Naomi unable to pull Spotty back and they both disappeared down them in full canter. I managed to steer Pudding to the side and literally jumped off, while he to stepped to and fro next to me, dripping in sweat. I looked back and I could see the others were catching up to us and thankfully soon arrived on the scene. Blondie was quick to admonish me

"You never leave the group; it can make a horse bolt." Agreed. I would never do that again.

Pudding didn't seem to be that much calmer, so I decided that I really wasn't going to ride him down the steps. Holding the reins firmly, trying to keep his head on a slight turn and my elbow pushing his shoulder, the two of us battled our way to the bottom. There was only one mounting block before home, so I either got on now or walked it. I decided to get on, and off we all went. Once we had reversed our route back up the main road we waived goodbye to Blondie and proceeded on our way. Pudding still hadn't calmed down and neither had Spotty. As we turned into a quiet residential road, Spotty decided to canter off and for the second time that day Pudding decided to chase her. Naomi finally managed to turn Spotty into a small side-track while I, in turn, managed to swing Pudding into a double driveway where I made him do circles in an attempt to calm him down. My apologies to the family eating their Sunday dinner who sat open-mouthed as a white beastie circled just feet away from their dining room window.

So far, I had managed to keep my cool. Although my head was racing, I tried very hard to keep focussed on the moment and not the fact that I was feeling really quite scared now. Ruth and Janet caught up and neither of their horses seemed the slightest bit bothered by any of the antics which had been going on around them.

Janet was quick to say, "Caroline, loosen your reins." I promptly did, and slotted in behind her horse, while Naomi steered Spotty behind Ruth's. It was still another mile or so to hack home and it felt like an eternity. I kept repeating to myself, "You'll soon be there; you'll soon be there." And eventually we were. I was astonished that Pudding was still feisty and full of life considering we had been hacking for over four hours. When I turned him out in the field, he galloped off and did several circuits before stopping.

Janet and Ruth became my mentors that day. When I returned to the stable, they were waiting for me.
"Now, don't over think this Caroline. That was a one-off, Pudding is normally as good as gold" said Ruth.

"Come out on a hack first thing tomorrow and put this to bed. Or it will hang over you and you won't want to ride him."

And they were absolutely right. The three of us headed off for a short hack the following morning and Pudding was his usual laid back and chilled out self. There was no drama. No speed. No events.

Life settled into a lovely routine of pleasant hacks followed by drinks and a chat We had whiskey with our tea and brandy with our coffee and lots of laughs with our chatter. It was on one of these mornings that we all decided we were perchers – sitting perched on the front of our saddles. Janet said she knew this was an absolute fact, as her sheepskin saddle cover was moulded into the perfect cast of her phoophoo. It made sense to us that should we ever need to marry again, any prospective partner should be asked to ride on Janet's sheepskin, so we could make a proper assessment of him. And if we won the lottery, well we would buy a supreme dressage horse, enter her in all the top events and call her Tena Lady.

You're late

I was enjoying Pudding more and more. He had moments when he was demonstrably affectionate, came when I called him and was a comedy act in his stable. If you were even a fraction late to turn him out in the morning, he would pull over everything he could reach - I would walk down the aisle to his stable and be greeted with the wheelbarrow on its side, every fork and brush on the floor and all his rugs pulled off the rail and laid in a heap.

There were frequent occasions when I felt completely taken over by affection for him. Many an evening I would bring him from the field and just stroke him. There seemed to be a bond that was formed from just gently letting my hand slide down the soft warm fur on his neck, whilst he nickered in approval. This was very different to anything I had experienced before, there was an invisible energy connecting us both, it was becoming an absolute lesson in living in the moment. I found myself completely content.

I did wonder whether I really meant anything to him or whether it was all in my mind and then came the confirmation. It was late December and our eldest daughter was back from Australia for a month over Christmas. Phil had decided that the whole family was going to New York for a week, our first family holiday in years. We had a magical time, with so many laughs and we came back in a real Christmassy mood.

While I was away, Pudding was on full livery and I had received word that he was fine. All the same, on my return I couldn't wait to see him and drove to the livery yard within an hour of getting back. It was now late afternoon as I headed towards the paddock where he stood bunched with his field mates. As soon as he saw me he sprang into action and trotted towards the gate whinnying. He nuzzled me and seemed delighted to see me. It honestly melted my heart. He meant the world to me, I was so touched that I clearly meant something to him.

It was around this time that I made the decision I really wanted the ability to get out and about, so I needed transport of my own. I spent a long time researching the options. If I got a trailer then I would have no ongoing MOT, tax or servicing, but they are notoriously harder to drive, and I would need to change my car for one with a bigger engine. Considering I do high mileage, that would mean I am spending the majority of my time driving a less economical car, which would cost me a lot more in fuel. A small van seemed like the best option for me. I chatted to Ria and we decided to combine a planned trip around the legendary Somerford Park with Amy as my instructor and loading practice with Pudding in her beautiful new van. Ria arrived with Chrissy, they parked, opened the horse loading area and I brought Pudding out.

It is probably worth mentioning that Highlands originate from the Scottish Highlands and they are extremely strong horses and very well built. They have been bred over the years to carry dead stags home from a hunt and can comfortably take an eighteen-stone weight on their back. So when they don't want to do something, believe me, you have some fight on your hands.

As we walked across the yard to the van, Pudding was sniffing the air madly and as soon as we got to the van, he dug his heels in and said no. The more we attempted to get him in, the more belligerent he became. He swung round nearly knocking the side bar off its hinges and reversed off the side of the ramp. We took a break while I walked him around the ménage and had a chat with him. He seemed nice and calm until we approached the van again when he stiffened up and fought every further attempt to load him. Not wanting to distress him, I cancelled the trip and returned him to his stable.

That evening I sat and pondered at some length. When I had been to view him, I had seen him walk in and out of a trailer at least five times as they demonstrated that he had no problems with loading. I had spoken to the transporter who had originally taken him to Cornwall and he said he was as good as gold. What was the problem now?

I concluded it could be one of three things. Either the trip to Cheshire had been so horrendous he was simply not prepared to travel again; or he thought I was moving him to a new owner; or finally, he knew how to load in a trailer, but a small 3.5 tonne side loader was beyond his comprehension. There was nothing I could do about the first two options at this point, but I could about the third. I began looking for a particular type of van, one that loads in the same way as a trailer, with a ramp at the back, two forward facing stalls and a side ramp for the exit.

I joined Horseboxes for Sale on Facebook and all the usual websites to hunt for what I wanted, within the budget I had set. Most were either too expensive, had no payload or were ancient. Then to my delight up popped exactly the van I was looking for, an ex-BT van with 148K mileage in good condition, with a long service history and a Ifor Williams cargo for the horses. It goes without saying there was a trip involved, so one murky Sunday afternoon my husband and I set off for Yorkshire.

When we arrived, we were greeted by Geoff and Sarah, a lovely local couple, she was bright and breezy, and a keen horsewoman and he was the grafter, with hands like shovels and teeth like tombstones. She chirped away, while he nodded silently, making no attempt to sell the van which would have made no odds anyway, as I have a deep suspicion of anyone who tries too hard to sell me something. There were a few areas which on closer inspection needed seeing to, there was no gate on the right-hand side of the ramp and no mat at the bottom of the partition, but otherwise it was perfect.

It was decided we would go for a test drive, leaving our female host behind the remaining three of us piled into the van. Now my husband is a well-built man and Geoff could certainly fill a seat, so it was very cosy in the cab to say the least. With Geoff driving off we trundled, down to an industrial estate where we swopped places and I jumped into the driver's seat and pulled on the seatbelt which refused to budge. I can't remember the last time I drove anywhere without a seatbelt, but I was surprised to learn that Geoff never uses them. Looking at him, I could well imagine that his car could be written off and he would still walk away unscathed. After that small hiccup, we practiced corners, brakes, reversing, and all the usual light checking and tyre kicking that people who don't really know what they are looking for feel compelled to do. After a cup of tea, a check of the documents including the weighbridge certificate confirming the payload, we agreed to buy the van subject to a pre-purchase inspection and the seatbelt being fixed.

Once I was back home I set about the thankless task of trying to find someone who could do the inspection for me. They had to know about vans and engines obviously, but I needed someone who could check the horse area to ensure the floor and ramps were sound. After much trawling through the internet, I found a man who builds horseboxes, lived about forty-five miles away from the van and did pre-purchase inspections. He charged me £150 for the inspection and a further £90 for the travel. He only had one review, which was OK, but there was literally nobody else anywhere near. I now look back on this inspection with a great degree of mixed feelings, he did all the checks and sent pictures and comments via messenger. However, I later learned that he had taken his eight-year-old daughter with him and she sat in the van while he did the inspection – an inspection that did not involve actually driving the van at all. It is eight months on and I am still waiting for the written report! However, the van was sound and that was all I really needed to know. I agreed to buy, and Geoff drove it over the following evening.

So now I had transport, this was a liberating prospect. I drove it to the livery yard and decided that I would try loading Pudding in it, to see if he felt as excited about the opportunity to travel further abroad as I did. Well, he didn't. As we approached the ramp he applied the brakes and no amount of pressure on my beloved Monty Roberts head collar was moving him. I spent the next fifteen minutes trying this way and that, to no avail – the horse was not for loading.

Jonny had been watching me, he sauntered up and said,

"I bet you £50 that I'll have that horse loading in ten minutes."

I knew he would, so the bet was on; with a £10 wager, one pound for every minute. We moved the van next to a wall, had both the back ramp and the side ramp open and Jonny gathered Pudding, walking firmly to the van. I found it really frustrating that my horse just seemed to know that he could not prat around with him but felt free to royally take the mick with me. Pudding walked around calmly, halting at the bottom of the ramp staring into the van. Jonny picked up one of his hooves and placed it on the bottom of the ramp and then slowly they made their way up and into the cabin. After a very brief pause at the top for a carrot reward, they exited via the side ramp. Jonny repeated this exercise four times and each time Pudding went in with less and less hesitation, until he was just walking in without thinking. The whole process took seven minutes, unbelievable.

Finally, I now had the opportunity of doing one of the things that I had wanted to do for so long, even before I actually got a horse - the farm ride at Somerford Park. For those of you not familiar with this venue, it is an eighty-acre estate otherwise known as Horse Heaven. The summer and winter rides have purpose built sandy tracks which wind around a beautiful estate, with optional jumps and a wade through the river. The hub of the estate holds a dressage arena, jumping areas and a cross country course for eventers; this for serious horse people with horses that run into five, sometimes six figure sums.

I had been so disappointed when my original trip to Somerford fell through after Pudding refused to load into Ria's van. So it was with great excitement that a new trip was planned, and it would be my first venture out in my own new transportation. I was being escorted by Holly, a very experienced and takes no-messing rider, with a 17 hands high grey mare called Violet. The night before I could not sleep, the nerves kicked in and all I could see was a long parade of 'what if' scenarios, most of them involving an unpleasant ending. What If he was so excitable I couldn't control him, or stop him, or we galloped off – you get the picture. I was still awake at 3am in the morning, tired with a ball of tension in the pit of my stomach and a sense of impending doom.

Whilst I still had some nerves the following morning, I was nowhere near as frightened as the night before. I was also becoming well practised at the Fake It till you Make It response to life. I arrived at the yard with a smile, took twice as long as Holly to get ready, which was perfectly normal for me, loaded Pudding and followed Holly's van to our destination. As we drove through the gates and crawled along to the parking area, the whole place suddenly seemed twice as large as I had ever seen it. It was the week after Christmas and it looked like everyone had had the same idea, it was crazily busy. I parked and opened the ramp to be greeted by a horse who immediately started sniffing the air wildly, with eyes darting everywhere trying to ascertain where he was. Full of beans, he unloaded and moved endlessly round as I tried to tack him up, he was already excited by the number of horses and seemed giddy, ready for action. I knew he had hunted in his past and I was seriously hoping he didn't think that was what we were doing today.

Once tacked up it was time to mount and apparently, if you are a serious rider you mount from either the floor or the horse ramp. I cannot think of any occasion when I have had to lift my leg to waist height, so I was pretty sure that was not going to happen. I tried to get Pudding next to the ramp, so I could gain some height, but he was not playing ball, trying to mount a moving object would tax the best of riders and Pudding was not for standing still. In the end I stood on the ramp and jumped at him, so in the most undignified manner possible, with me still half-hanging off the saddle as we walked off, I did manage to scramble on-board. We made our way to the ride entrance and waited our turn.

As we stood watching, one magnificent beast after another shimmied past us. Horses shone with gleaming coats, arched necks, polished tack and immaculate riders. To a man, they all looked down on this little hairy pony with an air of disgust. With similar outlook to a Jack Russell, who will take on dogs twice its size and seem to have no concept that it is actually a 'small dog'; the Mighty Midget had no concept that he did anything but fit in perfectly and backed that up with some flirty moves on one particular mare. We pranced along behind her until the owner had clearly had enough of this nonsense and trotted off.

Holly proved to be the perfect partner for a first visit to Somerford. Her mare was calm and completely unaffected by her surroundings and Holly provided valuable instruction and encouragement. It occurred to me that picking your riding partners for key events can make the difference between success and failure. We were definitely going to succeed today. We arrived at the water, a slopping descent into a little lake for horses to wade through or jump into from steps if you were feeling brave. I waded, turned around and did it again. This was probably the first time I took a full breath since we set off. Pudding was not quite as light on his feet and seemed to be settling down. We continued onto the steps, a steep set of three steps into a bowl and then back up on the other side with three steps of similar size.

"Let's do the steps," said Holly, so off I went, quickly realising that I was on my own.

I looked back as Pudding dropped down one step after another, to see Violet refusing point blank to descend. Now this is when the fun started. As we got to the bottom we could see the track which ran around the bowl at the top and a group of Pony Clubbers were shooting past, taking a jump or two on their way. Pudding became really animated, spinning one way then another to try and get to grips with what was happening above us. With my heart pounding, I decided we had better get back up as quickly as possible, so I pointed him to the stairs and up we flew. At the top there were groups of horses everywhere, all engaged in high-energy pursuits, which made Pudding dance about ready for action. Eventually, Holly appeared and quickly escorted us away from this hive of activity to the quiet of a woodland track.

It dawned on me that we had done less than a mile of what is an eight-mile route. I had better get this together or we would be in for a confidence busting couple of hours. I loosened the reins and tried to relax. Thankfully, this seemed to do the trick and my little grey equine firework began to relax as well. We had a joyful mile or so walking and trotting through the glorious parkland and rounded towards Canter Hill. Most of you will be well aware that hills are a great place to practice a canter, it wears the horse out and you are less likely to go bombing off when you reach the top.

We paused at the bottom while Holly said, "Just relax and let him go."

Within a split second of her signalling to go, Pudding was off and we were galloping full pace up the hill. I felt like I had been propelled out of a cannon. It is hard to describe the power of a horse in full gallop, it really is quite astonishing. You feel their strength and power as they surge forward, and it is echoed in the thunderous sound of the hooves on the ground below. I was relieved that it was surprisingly easy to ride. Scary, but fun. However, old habits die hard and like a child with a comfort blanket, I still preferred having one hand on the saddle strap.

A second or two later Holly appeared, unruffled by her controlled canter and was
genuinely surprised at how fast Pudding could go. Not as surprised as me, I can tell you. We took in one further hill that day with the same G-force rendering ascent to the top. I actually found myself urging him to go faster and he responded with heart popping speed; as though all the energy he had stored up suddenly found

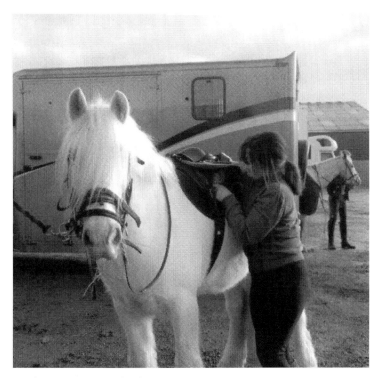

My first trip to Somerford

an outlet. When we finally stopped at the top he was covered in sweat, but there was a magical moment when we seemed so connected, having both enjoyed that adrenaline rush together.

By the time we got back to the van my pony looked like he had been dragged through a hedge backwards. Covered in sweat and mud, his forelock had parted and somehow made its way behind his ears – so he looked like some strange Lord of the Rings elfin character.

He was pretty shattered but still distracted by everything around him, so it took three attempts and a lunge line around the bum before we got him back into the van. Back at the yard he was still a little wired when we placed him back in his stable, but eventually he settled down to the serious business of eating hay.

Later that evening I messaged the teenager who had owned him originally to let her know how we had got on. The couple who had sold me Pudding had provided her contact details, as she had desperately wanted to keep in touch with whoever had Pudding, as he had been such a huge part of her life for over six years. I found having her as a source of information invaluable. I have spoken to her many times to ask her about his hay fever, loading, clipping, occasional stubbornness and a whole range of other stuff. I sent her pictures and video footage, so she could see how he was and today I was letting her know that he had moved like a rocket. I laughed at her response

"It's quite shocking when he does it. You really don't expect it from such a chunka".

Chapter Five

Spurred on by the success of my outing I decided I would set myself another challenge. I booked an Intro B dressage test at the local equestrian centre and gave myself four weeks to get ready. Preparation is key, or so they say, so I ordered a laminated copy of the test complete with little pictures showing where you should be and what you should be doing at each stage. Picturing our ménage at the yard I would close my eyes and visualise the route, until I knew it off by heart. I had intended to practice twice a week, but that did not quite work out. After a few attempts in the ménage I found it was the day of the test and I have never felt less ready for anything.

Thankfully, my sister agreed to accompany me and brought her usual sunshine to the proceedings. At the crack of dawn, we dragged Pudding out of his stable into the van and pottered along in a blur of chatter and giggles.

Once we had arrived and parked up it occurred to me that I had no idea how Pudding would respond, hopefully not in the animated fashion of Somerford Park where he spent the first fifteen minutes as wired as a crack cocaine addict who had just had a hit. He picked his way down the ramp with his usual air sniffing routine and I walked him around to let him see where we were and what was happening. Now this is why it's a good idea to buy a horse who has done things, he seemed to acknowledge the event with all the ease of a seasoned pro. For my part I was practicing a skill I had been using for years, whenever I had a big pitch or important meeting I would try and switch the emotions off and focus on whatever it was I had to do. Today I simply had to remember which way to go.

Once mounted, we headed into the warm up arena where he was willing and responsive, this was going really well. My name was called and in we went, this was it. To my horror, I realised that the ménage lettering was back to front, not the way I had rehearsed it in my mind; instead of entering at the bottom and then turning right I would be entering at the top and turning left. There was also a dawning realisation that I had no idea what the dressage etiquette was; do I go around the outside first, do I just swing into action or should I wait for a signal? We trotted round and began to turn to go in when there were two peeps of the horn and I was called over by the usher. Apparently, the adjudicator did not like the position of my saddle and felt it was too far back, I must make my way out of the arena and sort it before being called back.

I had been totally zoned into doing my test and was now a little flustered at being called out of the arena by an usher, who stood watching me struggling to adjust the saddle forward and pull the girth strap as high as I could get it. Normally I have a gel saddlecloth to help keep the saddle in place, but I had bought a lovely one for the test, which looked divine but had no grip at all. I stood there using every ounce of strength to pull the straps, but I just could not get them as far as the next hole. Eventually the usher stepped in and had the whole thing secured in seconds. We nodded at each other, she was letting me know 'that is how you do it' and mine was in reverence at the extraordinary power her fingers possessed. If I ever find out her name is Jamie Summers I would not be the least bit surprised.

Back to the warm up arena, a quick circuit then back in to do my test. Pudding was a superstar, he seemed to know exactly what was expected of him and kept his pace, performing beautifully. We didn't manage an outline, but considering I was working with a ménage that was back to front and it was our first test, I thought we did pretty well. I saluted at the end and there was a cheer from my faithful supporters who had watched from the side. Feeling pretty pleased that I had at least given it a go, we plodded back to the van, past all the perfectly paced riders and arched necked horses. I hoped I wasn't placed last; really hoped, and that my score would be at least 50 percent.

Phew, we did it

We packed up and dropped Pudding off at the yard, as there were that many entrants it would be at least another hour if not more before everyone had taken their turn, let alone got their scores. I went home, changed and we drove back later that afternoon with Phil spending the entire trip trying to prepare me for the worst

"Don't be upset if the score is not that high, you took part and that is what counts."

With apprehension, we walked into the café where all the score sheets were lay across a table, after much rummaging we found it. I was absolutely stunned, 66.7 percent and seventh position. How I love that horse!

Within no time at all Spring was upon us and the weather was beginning to lift. I had a real desire to get out and about, so I persuaded Ruth to do a little hack I had researched. She was bringing her mare and we planned to park up in a small country park a couple of miles away and hack down a bridleway to the pub and back.

This would be the first time Pudding had travelled in the van with another horse, but while he could be a little resistant to going in, generally he had been good to load. By now, I was feeling so much more confident about being around horses, so I volunteered to load Ruth's mare. With the magic head collar on I walked briskly to the van and straight up the ramp and the mare seemed quite surprised to find herself suddenly stood in a stall in a horsebox. The same thing happened with Pudding, he was in before he fully realised that he was not in his usual position and he was sharing with a mare who, up till now, couldn't stand the sight of him.

We closed up and set off, arriving at our destination about ten minutes later. Ruth was nervous, she had a mare who reacts badly to tractors, with a propensity to take off on the inside of the group to get as far away from the machine as possible. She also had a history of kicking out at Pudding whenever he got too close, usually his fault, as he had a history of sticking his nose up her bottom. Yet today, with the absence of any other mare to partner with, she made Pudding her new best friend and stuck to him like glue. I had to admit that I was wondering how we would get on. Up to now, Pudding had only led the hacking group for a short space of time, but today he was going to be in front the whole way.

Thankfully, Pudding did not share my concern, he seemed very relaxed when he got off the van, so I walked him around the car park giving him a chance to see where he was. Using a wooden bench as a mounting block I climbed on and off we went. With his head held high he gallantly led us down the road and up the track to the large gate, which marked the start of the bridle path. Now this was no ordinary gate, it was one designed to ensure that only the most determined rider would get through – it opened towards you and had a fence at the side to stop the horse from falling into the cattle grid and a hedge on the other. Yet it didn't matter which way you approached it, there just did not seem to be enough room to pull the gate open and manoeuvre the horse round before you lost your grip and it snapped shut. After ten exhausting minutes and many, many attempts, there seemed nothing for it but to get off, get both horses through and somehow remount on the other side. It quickly became clear that there was literally nothing that you could stand on to help you get back on, so in desperation I lowered a stirrup as low as it would go and levered myself on. No matter how hard I fiddled with them, the stirrups then remained at different lengths for the entire hack.

The sun was shining, the daffodils were out, and we descended through a lush green valley, with a glistening meandering river at the bottom. Chatting merrily, it was the perfect hack and we were both enjoying ourselves enormously. We negotiated two more gates on our way, whilst problematic they were not quite as spiteful as the first one. Once at the pub we decided on a little sherry before working our way back. We will be forever grateful to the group of ramblers using the path that day, who having dispersed themselves along the route were all perfectly placed to open all three of the gates which had caused so many problems on the journey out. As we dismounted our little cup of happiness overflowed, we had done it without event or injury!

I walked the mare onto the van without any issue and grabbed Pudding who he clearly had other ideas. As we approached the ramp he pulled back with such force I lost hold of him and he trotted off across the car park to a stretch of grass and started eating. I couldn't believe it. I walked over, grabbed the lead rope and tried again; exactly the same thing happened. By now, we were becoming the entertainment and groups of onlookers who had only had the ducks on the lake to amuse them, now turned their full attention to us. Feeling the weight of responsibility on my shoulders, I was determined to get this horse on to the van. Now, there is an old saying that if you do the same thing you've always done, then you will get the same thing you've always got. At this point I had not stopped to consider whether the pressure I had was enough. If I had, then

I would have realised that I had hooked the lead rope onto the neutral ring and not the pressure point – so no matter how hard I pulled, it was having no effect at all.

Not realising this, I stormed towards the van with Pudding in tow and used every ounce of strength to pull him in; which was met with a horse using every ounce of his strength to resist. Obviously, the horse won – and he was taking no chances on a repeat attempt, so he trotted off, through the gate and out of the park. My heart stopped, there was a busy A road at the end of the lane and he was now in real danger of getting run into by a car. I ran after him and found him twenty metres down the road. I slowed to a saunter as I knew he would move forward if I approached too quickly, and sure enough he did decide to walk forward but thankfully stood on the lead rope and brought himself to a halt. I grabbed him and was so thankful that nothing had happened to him, I made no attempt to tell him off. We walked back together and back into the car park and our ever-increasing audience.

While we had been gone, Ruth's mare had heard all the commotion behind her and started to get agitated in the van, so Ruth had no choice but to bring her off until Pudding was back safe and sound. There we both stood, horses in hand, emotionally expended and with an arc of onlookers.

"What are we going to do?" asked Ruth.
"I've no idea," I replied.

We tied the horses up and began to think of our options; of course, let's get Jonny. As neither of us had his phone number, we called everyone we could think of who knew him and eventually we got the message back to say he was on his way.

"We're going to have to go now," said a disappointed pair of old ladies who had not moved an inch from the side-lines since the drama began. "we should have been at our lunch date twenty minutes ago."

After what felt like an eternity to us, but was actually about ten minutes, Jonny pulled into the car park grinning from ear to ear. We stood there like a pair of bookends while he loaded both horses within minutes, only to find himself confronted by two rather emotional ladies. We couldn't stop hugging him in gratitude, with eyes full of happy tears. On our way home, we pondered how the hell he had managed to do it so easily, clearly Cheshire's answer to the horse whisperer.

The following week I decided to take the matter in hand and began what would turn into months of loading practice. Every morning I would open the van, put his breakfast on the floor and walk him in. It did not escape my notice that he had no problems whatsoever walking in and out of the van when food was involved, he practically raced me in there on some days. I had already concluded that this horse was razor sharp when it came to working out an angle. I would need to be just as cute in keeping on top of him.

Janet was upset to miss out on a trip. Especially as, loading excluded, we had enjoyed a really great time. Spring was in full force and we felt we wanted to get out and enjoy it, so we settled on a beautiful hack around The Cloud; a glorious outcrop of rocks with views spanning three counties. As the destination was only fifteen minutes away and the van could only hold two horses we decided that I would drive Ruth, Janet and their horses to the car park, they would wait there for me and I would return with Pudding. It was one of the first glorious days of the year, with temperatures in the late teens and cool fresh breezes.

Once we were all assembled together and tacked up, we made our way down the lanes to the bridle path that would take us up and around the side of this elevation. The horses seemed to enjoy the fresh scenery and having to apply their brains to work out the best footing down the stony track. Pudding was my hero, as usual, often taking the lead and happy to escort his little harem past any obstacle which caused them unease. Once we had completed half our circuit we found ourselves on narrow country lanes, with a deep valley to one side and romantic country cottages dotted along the other. Hawks soared in the valley beyond and the air was full of birdsong, it was breathtakingly beautiful. We soon decided that this was our favourite hack so far and a pub short of being absolutely perfect. On the descent, the dwellings started to get closer and closer together, some cute postcard cottages and other quite palatial spreads. It really is so much fun on a horse, you can see so much more than when you are in a car; directly over hedges and into front rooms, gardens and when the building is really old, the bedroom as well.

Once back at the van we dismounted, packed the tack away and began the business of loading Pudding. Unbeknownst to me, he decided he was not loading today. As I walked him towards the van, with one deft jerk he pulled free and trotted off through a narrow gap in the fence and rooted himself in the picnic area, eating grass. Janet stood at the back of the car park, clearly the whole thing was greatly disturbing her nerves. Ruth was a little more gung-ho, while I grabbed the lead rope and walked him back, she flanked him on the other side and we frog marched him into the van. What on earth? After months of practising, I knew he had not one jot of concern about going into the van, so I began to consider that there may be something else. Once all were safely back at the yard I had a closer look at the van and wondered if the head of the bolts securing the gate panels might be an issue, as there seemed to be a lot of tail hair wrapped around them. I examined his tail, and parting the hair discovered a pink and sore area on his dock at the level of the gate. Right then.

As someone who had grown up watching Blue Peter, I knew how to make a thing or two. On receipt of my eBay orders of Pleather and foam, I constructed a rather fetching padded panel which attached onto the top gate strut. After changing all the bolts for ones with flatter, rounder heads; I glued the panel over the top and felt sure the problem would now be resolved. Whilst Pudding can sometimes hesitate before going in since my little intervention, I have not had any repeat of his escape artist routine.

Someone once told me the only way you could learn to ride was to put in the hours in the saddle. While the weeks were spent either practicing in the ménage or hacking, I did begin to feel things were falling into place. By now I was getting a handle on how Pudding was going to react to things. There was no chance of him bolting, bucking or rearing; that simply wasn't his thing. If he spooked, he would either judder on the spot, or if it was something he suddenly spotted at the side of him, he would jump sideways. Now and again, he would back away from something ahead, but that was something that had started in recent months and I suspect he picked it up from watching some of the other horses do it. Thankfully, with some strong encouragement from me, we were able to get past anything that bothered him.

One of the lovely things about having your own horse, is that not only do you get to understand them, but they do the same with you. I am a novice rider, with an extensive range of dodgy signals, but amazingly Pudding now knows what they are and what I am trying to ask him to do. So he gets on and does it.

I wondered what it would be like if I fell off, it is a huge obstacle in your mind until it actually happens, after that, it is not something you want, but you don't fear it in the same way. The first time I fell off was while we were in walk, in fact, of the three occasions I have come off, they have been while we were walking. I was with Janet and Ruth hacking along a strip of grass which ran parallel to a road. There must have been something in the hedge that startled Ruth's mare, as she suddenly jumped sideways, and like a set of dominos they all went. Ruth was off and so was I. It all happened in a split second and I felt only slight discomfort from where I had hit the ground. We stood there for a minute or two in stunned silence, not quite believing what had just happened.

Janet , who was still firmly sat in her saddle, looked horrified

"Are you alright? Are you hurt? Are you alright?"
"I'm fine" shouted Ruth
"Me too" I replied

Ruth was trying desperately to figure out what had caused it

"I didn't see anything. There was nothing there"

We concluded that the mare must have seen something, maybe a plastic bag in the hedge or a bird moving, either way the two of us were off, covered in mud down one side of our body with no visible means of getting back on.

I look back on the event and the only real discomfort I felt was the walk of shame, covered in mud escorting my horse on foot down the pavement to the amusement of passing motorists.

I decided that I would like to improve and for some reason it made perfect sense at the time to learn to jump. Nothing too big, to be honest, neither Pudding or I are built to be airborne. The rationale was simple – if I ever found myself in a spot of bother and we were going to have to jump something to get out of it, then I would prefer to know what to do.

I enrolled the help of Jonny and we began. Our first task was pretty straightforward, we were to circle the ménage and then trot through some jump wings, using the poles on the floor for guidance. Round and round we went, focussing on building up a little more speed and being a little more accurate when aiming for the centre of our imaginary jump. Without any warning, whilst I had my back to him doing my little circuit, Jonny erected two cross poles. I circled towards the jump and spotted them which gave me a start and I nearly bottled it. He was shouting for me to keep going so we trotted towards them and went over them without it feeling like we had even left the ground. I decided that it was OK to breathe again and couldn't believe how easy that had been. For the next twenty minutes we repeated the exercise, to my absolute disbelief and joy we were jumping cross poles and loving every minute of it.

This was exciting stuff, during the next week I would regularly set up a couple of cross pole jumps, grab Pudding and have my very own happy hour.

It was at this point I became more acquainted with the teenage whose stable was on the other side of mine. Chrissy was quiet, even a little shy, but lovely in every way. She wanted to do things, but had little confidence in her own, quite considerable abilities. Her cob was a barrel, young and prone to getting very excited when faced with new situations, which put her off wanting to attempt anything new. Chrissy explained that they had once tried to do a course of jumps at the same equestrian centre I had done my dressage test, but her horse had become so excitable she ended up shouting at him in fear and frustration. It was only Jonny's intervention from the side-lines, shouting directions at her, that pulled her together.

We would often chat about what we would like to do, and it was during one of these conversations that we decided we would hire the jump arena and ask Jonny to give us a lesson in there. It would give her horse the opportunity to use the venue without the pressure of a competition and I needed all the practice I could get. The evening arrived and in the fading light we loaded the horses and arrived nearly an hour early for our lesson. As soon as the clock struck six, we were into the arena, Jonny was quickly changing the jumps from one metre plus, down to cross poles, while Chrissy and I trotted our horses round to warm them up. Pudding, as the seasoned pro didn't bat an eyelid at anything. We trotted past the viewing stand, the café, the side wall with the stables on the other side; while Chrissy had to make a few circuits before her gelding decided that there was nothing to be worried about.

Jonny announced that we would go one at a time, so Chrissy went first and with a rhythmic collected canter covered the whole course perfectly. My turn. The time was now around 6:30 p.m. and Pudding would normally have been in his stable with his PJs on, as far as he was concerned this was bedtime and there was no chance of him suddenly bursting into life. We trotted round at a slow but steady pace and jumped our cross poles to the sound of Jonny shouting 'Wakey, Wakey'. After several turns, our hour was up, and we returned to the yard feeling quite proud of ourselves.

A few weeks later a message went out to all liveries, there would be an event to raise money for Comic Relief which would include a jump round. I responded, if it included cross poles then count me in. Further details emerged - there would be a raffle and a cake stall. Yum. Now, co-incidentally, a couple we had known for years made contact. She had an allotment and desperately wanted some manure for it, would she be able to collect some? We arranged for them to come on the Saturday and collect as much manure as she wanted, they could have tea and cake whilst watching me jump.

The day arrived, and I went to get Pudding from the field. It always made me giggle to see him in his rug. I needed to buy a 6'3" as he was so wide, but that size is normally worn by much taller horses than Pudding, so the rug always went down past his knees. He looked like the kid at school who had to wear his big brother's jumper.

He was his usual placid self and calmly munched on hay while I groomed him and tacked him up. He looked gorgeous, and like a proud mother, I couldn't wait to show him to my friends. They arrived and briefly stroked him, commenting that he looked much more handsome in real life and then moved on to a general catch up. I forget sometimes that your horse may mean the world to you, but not necessarily mean anything at all to someone else.

The call came, it was our turn. I walked Pudding into the ménage and we did a warm up, but it was pretty clear that he was not in the mood today. It was extremely hot, and he just could not be bothered. With a line of people, including my friends, propped against the fence as I began my round with a horse that was moving only one notch up from a walk. While I was working overtime, kicking and urging him on, he sauntered along and more or less walked over the poles. At one point he stopped dead in front of the jump and like Delaney's Donkey, he wouldn't budge. This was really embarrassing and when the offer came to try again, I politely declined.

Airborne!

I knew that I needed more work on my jumping technique, but right now it seemed like it would be good for both of us to get out and do something we both enjoyed, so I found a fun ride for the following weekend and roped in Janet and Holly.

So, with one extra at the last minute, our merry little party set off for the Marbury Park Fun Ride.

I was happy to lead the way as I knew where Marbury Park was, and my van was much smaller and nippier than Holly's lumbering seven and a half tonner. As always, I was very mindful that I am carrying two horses, so I never do more than thirty miles an hour and take the corners at a glacial pace; much to the annoyance of the mile-long string of motorists who gather behind me. With Janet sat next to me in the cab we entered Marbury Park and felt a slow rising sense of alarm that there was not one single horsebox in the car park. We found the instructions on the phone, and to our horror, the ride was not at this Marbury Park but another one of the same name based in Shropshire. I ask you, why on earth would give your grand estate the same name as the another one just down the road? Really!

We decided to phone Holly and picked up the phone to find numerous messages left by the plus one on her behalf, telling us to slow down and wait for her. Even though I was only doing thirty miles an hour, Holly's van rarely went faster than 20, so we had clearly frustrated her when she felt we were disappearing out of sight. By the time she cornered into the car park you could literally see the steam coming out of her ears. This was entirely my fault and I would need to apologise, but I was going to give it a good few minutes before I went anywhere near that lorry.

She was clearly quite cheesed off, but we decided to make the most of it. The fun ride was another hour drive away, which seemed too far as the horses had already been travelling for an hour, so we settled on Somerford Park instead. Both Janet and I were excited and apprehensive at the same time. She had not been before and had no idea what to expect, and me, because I had been before and knew exactly what to expect. As fate would have it, this was a bank holiday weekend, so I was visiting the ride for the second time when it was jam packed full of riders.

We squeezed into a space in the car park, unloaded and set off. Pudding knew exactly where he was and was already skipping along, we embraced the water at pace and then turned the corner to be greeted by a small log which I had walked past last time, but I now felt able to jump this time round. Holly's plus one went first, she was a very proficient teenage rider on a fast

Arab who flew over the jump with ease. Pudding and I made a fast trot up to the log, over and then a canter on until he calmed down and stopped a short while later. The plus one had already backtracked and was jumping it again, so I decided I would as well. As we made our way back, we levelled with the log just as the Arab was jumping it, Pudding swung round to see what was happening and I found myself propelled forward. He then decided he would eat some grass, lowered his head and the neck I was holding onto was now tilted towards the ground and I proceeded to slide down it like a small child on a baby slide. The floor was wet with mud and I was covered in it.

My second involuntary dismount completed, I used the log to remount, caked in evidence of my fall. I felt slightly relieved that I was not the only one having an eventful afternoon as we passed a man dripping in water walking his equally soaked ride back towards the stables.

"The river's deep," he chirped as he passed.

As we approached the steps, Pudding got giddy again, he must have thought we were going down – not a chance. We proceeded on with groups of riders in front, behind and passing us. There were horses everywhere, and it made ours excited and eager to join in. Janet looked almost ashen, but she remained firmly in her saddle and her mare seemed less bothered than the others at the excitement around her. We approached the hill riders normally let their horses canter up and after a discussion decided we would let ours burn off some excess energy and do the same. Pudding and I were at the back of the party, when we started at least, but with the same lightning speed as last time, as soon as one horse started to go

Pudding was off like a rocket. The thing that struck me as we hurtled up the hill, was the difference it makes when you have a group of horses bunched together so close you could reach over and touch another rider. It felt like the 12.30 at Chepstow races. If we were going to canter again, then I did not want to be stuck in the middle.

Once at the top we proceeded along our route, the newly opened summer ride which gave us the opportunity to go into the river. Janet hung back, but the rest of the party dropped down the bank into the swirling green waters. We waded along with water just below our stirrups and poor Pudding seemed a tad more submerged than the others. His head was lowered towards the water and he seemed deeply intrigued by the experience. We made our way back up the bank accompanied by the noise of water running off our horses like the sound of a large man emerging from a bath. It had cooled them down in every sense and we covered the next few miles in a slow and steady fashion.

We were coming toward the last section of the ride and had one last hill we could canter up. Collectively we decided that we wanted to, so with the Arab leading us on, off we went. As usual, Pudding and I were placed at the back and, as usual, Pudding took off. This time I directed him towards the outside of the group and as we rounded the corner at the top, we had moved into second position. Our plus one had signalled to her horse to keep going and she was heading off along the track in full gallop, with Pudding in hot pursuit. Janet was unable to stop her mare and found herself now being propelled along against her will.

"Please make it stop," I could hear her shout behind me.

I signalled to Pudding that I wanted him to stop, very unsure whether I had any brakes myself. It took a minute or two, but he eventually conceded, and we drew to a halt. Janet was visibly shaken and said, "I really didn't like that." Truth be told, whilst the gallop was always an adrenaline rush, I would have preferred it to be on my terms, so I am not sure I enjoyed it either. Janet's leg had narrowly missed the tree on the turn and she had been hemmed in with no room for manoeuvre, this had distressed her before we began our flat racing, so it was no wonder she was pretty shaken up by the time we finally stopped.

Later, when we were loaded and on the way home, we both said that had not been the day we had imagined and perhaps we would leave it a while before doing Somerford again.

Chapter Six

My yard is full of interesting people who enjoy a wide and extensive range of activities with their horses. There are a couple of ladies who are active endurance riders, membership of any endurance group allows you to ride long distances through private estates and parkland opened up exclusively to the organisation. You can have your horses time recorded and there is a leader board for those with the fastest times over the varying distances. Or you can simply do the ride for pleasure which is not timed or logged. I got a call from Ruth to say that there was one in our area whose route encompassed some parts we had previously hacked on when we went around The Cloud, and would I like to go. Hell yes.

Shortly before our ride I discovered a piece of knowledge which would prove to be invaluable to me. Monty Roberts talks about the one gift he wished he could give every horse rider and that is control of their breath. By keeping your breath slow and steady you can relax your horse, as they can see there is no need to panic as you obviously do not think there is any immediate threat anywhere. I resolved to practice this whenever the situation called for it and had no idea how quickly that would turn out to be.

It was another beautifully sunny day when we pulled into our nominated car park at the back of a large factory and collected our numbered tabards. Once mounted, we snaked our way out of the industrial estate and onto a disused railway track high above the surrounding countryside. Never one to miss an opportunity, we detoured round to a local pub and included a small stop and drink as part of today's ride. We remounted and continued in the way we thought we should be going, but before long it was clear that none of us had been following the map, or the blue arrows which had been sprayed onto roads and bushes along the route, so we did not have a clue where we were supposed to be heading. Ruth, who was born and raised in the area, came to the rescue and worked out the quickest way back to the railway track, so we headed down the hill back towards civilisation.

For anyone who has been riding a while, there are a whole heap of things that you have to consider when working out where you will or will not take your horse. Most horses are not overly fond of cows, donkeys, peacocks in full display, pay and display, road signs, pipes and so forth. But until we arrived upon it, no one had remembered that there was a quirky farm next to the road with an extensive collection of llamas. Pudding was leading our little party as we began to pass the farm and suddenly stopped becoming rigid with fear as three llamas craned over the wall and began to spit at him. I could actually feel him shaking beneath me.

Those first few moments felt almost frozen in time, we both stared at the Llamas trying to figure out what to do next. I kept urging him on and felt now was as good a time as any to practice the breathing thing. I slowed my breathing down and in a steady voice kept saying 'come on baby, come on you can so it'. Very gingerly he took a few pensive steps forward until we were level with the hairy horrors. I spotted a track on the other side of the road and signalled for Pudding to go there and with some pace he happily obliged. I sat there waiting for the others, but all I could hear was the clatter of hooves and shouting. Pudding was restless, pretty agitated but was prepared to follow my instruction and wait where he was.

The situation on the road was now mayhem. The mare behind Pudding had been struck by fear and simply refused to move, the one behind her had freaked out and bolted off into the bushes and the last mare, who had stopped quite a way back was now on a full meltdown as she was separated from her friends and didn't know what to do. Two riders had come off and they had yet to get the horses past the source of all the commotion, a wall that was now full of llamas who had all gathered to help their comrades spit at the large beasties invading their domain.

Cars had built up on either side of the road, reluctant to pass. Out of one of them jumped a lady who should have been wearing a red cape and knickers, for she turned out to be an equine psychologist and our superhero that afternoon. Using the same hidden magic Jonny uses, she took hold of the reins of each horse in turn, they immediately submitted to her authority and walked past the llamas without a single flinch to the lane where Pudding and I were waiting. Whoever you are, if you are reading this, then a heartfelt thank you from all the ladies you saved that afternoon.

Safely gathered together again, we all felt completely traumatised by what had just happened. I just did not feel like talking but a couple of others needed to offload their emotions and chatted for the next hour about the varying details of the event. The walk back to the vehicles was so very different to our outbound one, we had been excited and happy going out and all felt emotionally exhausted on our return.

Obviously, there was a great tale to tell the others when we got back to the yard and this adventure soon went down in Cob Club history as The Llama Drama.

It was a few days later I caught up with Chrissy. She was mortified when I recounted the events of the weekend and extremely thankful she hadn't gone, as she was not sure what her pony would have done.

'"You see, that is why I don't like hacking" she said firmly "he would have totally freaked out".

We were getting on famously and both felt ready, if not a little apprehensive, about pushing ourselves to the next level. During one of our customary chats we decided that we would enter the cross pole jumping competition held at our usual equestrian centre every Thursday evening. The following week we undertook reconnaissance and visited in the car to watch and make notes. Most riders arrived dead on the 5:30 p.m. start time, so if we got there at 4:30 p.m. we could be tacked, warmed up and done before there was any sort of crowd watching us. We walked the course of about twenty jumps and decided on our strategy.

The following week we were there at around twenty past four as I can be pretty anal about getting to things with plenty of contingency time. We registered, paid and began warming up. Pudding was not so interested, he managed a half decent trot during warm up, but the canter was under duress; he seemed to feel it very unfair that I was dragging him out *again* this close to his bedtime. By the time the event started, the livery yard owner and their family and friends had arrived and were stood next to the fence to watch us. Chrissy went first and did a perfect round. My turn.

We trotted in and I quickly realised they had changed the jump formation from last week. Honestly, they keep doing this to me! I signalled for Pudding to go and I actually felt him disengage, I was reliving Comic Relief all over again. With me working three times harder than the horse, we made our way round the course, thankfully he didn't knock any poles over and we were going so slowly Chrissy was able to shout directions from the side-lines in plenty of time me to take a leisurely look around for the next fence.

There are moments you never want to relive and that will remain firmly one of them. We had been doing so well when we practiced at home, but today was a gloriously shining example of a horse deciding they were not coming out to play and a rider unable to do a thing about it. I left the arena and circled round to walk back to the van just as the next rider sped in and proceeded to fly around the course. Chrissy disappeared to get food and I stayed with the horses, only to see her beaming face reappear a few minutes later.

"I've got 5th place and you've got 6th, isn't that great?"

How on earth was that possible? It transpires that two riders had fallen off and the group size that day was not that big. So there you have it, I can proudly display a rosette for doing a clear round at the slowest speed in Equine History.

What tickled me most from that evening was the difference in Chrissy between the journey there and the journey back. During our drive out, she was really nervous, and we kept repeating her magic word C-A-L-M in a long, drawn out manner. On the way back to the yard, we had the radio on full blast, she was singing along and doing full dance moves in her seat, which I have to say she was pretty damn good at. Nothing quite like pushing yourself out of your comfort zone and finding it was OK for lifting the spirits.

Once back at the yard I put Pudding back in his stable and we had a chat while he ate hay. In truth, I could never be mad at this horse. He looked after me so many times and I was pretty sure if I was a better rider then we would have flown around that course. I decided that it was all too easy being hard on yourself, much better to look how far we had come and be excited about the fact that there is still so much yet to conquer. At least we had tried for something and one day we will try and succeed.

Once I was back home I received a text from Janet, she had the following day off work and did I fancy a hack? Absolutely. We settled on a little hack around the

Exhausted after their exertions...

block. Once we were out and enjoying ourselves, we wanted to ride for a little longer.

"I wonder what's down there," said Janet, pointing to a country lane which spurred off from our normal route.
"I've no idea," I said, "do you want to look?"
"Oh, yes"

So off we went. It was quite an adventure, we went miles down the lane seeing little farms and cottages and even a stately manor house we had no idea even existed. We had been out for about two hours and there was still no sign of any side roads or tracks to help us circle back to the yard.

"do you have any idea where we are?" she asked
"none" I replied

We saw what could possibly be a track and took a turn onto it. We steadily climbed up the hill until we found ourselves at the rather splendid entrance to a sprawling mansion. Clearly, we had just spent twenty minutes on someone's private driveway. Making a quick turn before we were spotted we descended the way we came. We continued on our previous route and directly into a rainstorm.

"There has got to be some turning somewhere" Janet exclaimed "how long have we been out for?"
"Two hours"
"And what time is it now?
"Tomorrow" I replied.

After half an hour and another short rain storm later, we came to a T junction with a busy A road. We knew exactly where we were now, absolutely miles away from the yard. We had a choice, either turn back and retrace our steps which would be another two and half hours in the saddle, or hack down the track which ran next to the A road and be back in about hour. The horses were wet and tired, so we opted for the A road.

Now both of us had used short sections of this road many times before, but always on a Sunday morning when it is nice and quiet. We had no comprehension what lay in store for us that day as we crossed over and started down the track; the volume, size and speed of the traffic next to us was staggeringly relentless. Great big juggernauts flew past with such force it lifted the horses' manes in the air and blew us about in the saddle, it was like hacking down the side of a motorway. I will be forever grateful to those two amazing horses, with their heads set in the direction of home, who walked on with steely determination, completely unfazed by the traffic beside them. By the time we got back to the yard, both man and beast were utterly exhausted.

"I am absolutely drenched" declared Janet
"Indeed" I replied "even my knickers are wet".

We pondered the virtues of waterproof jodhpurs and the best way of getting a sheepskin saddle cover dry while finishing our jobs then setting off home for a hot toddy.

As summer approached, we found ourselves on summer livery. This is the glorious moment when your horses stay out 24/7 and you don't need to work your day around taking them out, bringing them in, mucking out and filling haynets and water buckets. It also marked a change in the hacking routine at the yard. Up to that point we hacked every weekend, as we were all there anyway to tend to the horses. As the weeks progressed, the routine of weekend hacks fell away, as people took the opportunity for a lie in or a weekend away. I desperately wanted to ride and was pleased that Janet was free that Sunday to go out for a hack. As fate would have it, her mare cracked her hoof during the week, so she was not going anywhere until it healed. That Saturday I was out with some friends enjoying a meal in a lovely local pub and suddenly out of nowhere came the thought that I could hack on my own. I played with the idea and by the time we were driving home, I had decided that was exactly what I was going to do.

Now I am a great believer in trying to set yourself up for success. There is a viewpoint in Neuro Linguistic Programming which argues that we are able to train our brain to deliver a desired outcome. The conscious mind sets goals and outcomes and our unconscious mind helps us get there. Like waking up with the solution to a problem you have been puzzling on for days. By tapping into our unconscious thoughts, we can play over the desired outcome again and again in our mind, like watching a video on repeat, until we can sense everything about how the outcome will work out. I had tried this technique before I viewed Pudding, I used it to replay events in a more positive way after the scary horse viewing experiences and I did it again that evening. Before going to sleep, I had played through the whole ride in my mind, how relaxed I would be, how laid-back Pudding would be and how the ride would go well without event.

It made sense that I should be up and out early, before the traffic began to build, just in case I got into trouble. So at 7 a.m. I drove into the yard, grabbed Pudding from the field and tacked up. Even though I felt nervous, I got into the saddle and we headed out of the yard and down the road. To my surprise, Pudding was completely laid back and seemed no different to how he normally is; not phased at all by being out on his own. I relaxed even more and began to enjoy myself.

The sun was shining, birds were singing and sitting there seemed like a glorious place to be. We pottered on down lanes, over bridges, past cattle in fields and round onto the bridle path. My biggest battle was in trying to keep Pudding moving, rather than stopping to eat. I guess that walking down a path with luscious vegetation at every turn is the equine equivalent of going through a drive-thru. We meandered on in calm enjoyment of each other's company, now and again we had a little trot and then back to a steady plod. As we rounded the final corner, past the church and onto the road back to the yard, it felt like we were such a tight little unit. There was trust between us and both us of really liked that. By the time I put Pudding back into the field, I was full of happiness. Not only had we done it, we'd smashed it.

We had been together now for nearly a year and I had lost count of all the times I had found myself well and truly out of my comfort zone. Riding a horse is a scary proposition, as someone pointed out to me, it's like playing football when the ball has a mind of its own. Talk to any group of riders for any length of time and they will tell you stories of horrific injuries inflicted by horses who have bolted, reared up or bucked someone off. You either have to be a great rider with confidence in your own ability to stay glued to the saddle or have some trust that you have a great horse who is prepared to look after you. Without doubt I sat in the latter camp. And the more we did together without anything unpleasant happening, the more I wanted to do.

If I could make my way around the block, then I could do something a bit bigger. I decided that I would venture out in the van for something a little more adventurous. The following Friday afternoon we set off for The Cloud, parking in the same place Pudding had done his great escape artist routine from. As we set off, Pudding seemed a little warier, this was a route he was not as familiar with, so his eyes were everywhere. We turned into the bridleway and began the climb, working our way steadily up and through the forest. After quite a stretch we hit the road, made our way down a short section before turning off again into woodland and tiny lanes. Pudding had completely settled and so had I. This felt amazing, we were working together, it wasn't about him following the horse in front, or taking confidence from others; he was listening to me and taking confidence from me and it was a complete joy to be part of our little team. By the time we got back to the car park, it was as though we had been doing it forever. He loaded without any bother and we made our way back. Without hesitation, I marked the time in my diary and determined I would do the same ride again the following Friday.

When Friday arrived we were there, unloaded and heading off down the lane. Now the first half of the hack went pretty much the same way as the last. However, as we turned onto the stretch of road Pudding saw something, who knows what, and did a big spook. We pressed on, but he was definitely more on edge today. As we made our way down one of the lanes he suddenly stopped, head aloft and slightly shaking. In the distance, I could hear the crack of gunfire and he seemed to be totally zoned in on it. I urged him on, but he was walking gingerly and still disturbed by the now constant rounds of shooting. I am not sure if what I did next was the right thing, but it seemed like the right thing at the time. I got off, grabbed him by the reins and walked him on. As we rounded the corner, the sound was deafening. It transpires that we were about to pass a Rifle Club and that evening it felt like every single member was in attendance to shoot the crap out of something. By the time we were level with the club, we could see the gunfire from the road and Pudding was snorting and prancing next to me. This was a big moment, so staying focussed, I kept my eyes forward as Fleur had told me and deliberately drew long breathes, keeping my shoulders down, making the odd audible sign. Pudding was transfixed on me, his eyes never moved from my face and I honestly think if I had panicked or shown fear, he would have been off. We marched on for about a mile before the sound of gunfire was beginning to fade. I found the nearest wall, stood on the top and remounted. Pudding walked at a much faster pace than normal and seemed to notice things today that he had happily passed last week without a second glance. But we got back to the van without any major incident and back home safe and sound.

I had to admit that I had not enjoyed the experience of being on my own with a frightened horse. I decided to leave it a little while before I went out on my own again.

On the whole we were progressing really well, but I felt I needed more lessons. During the week I had taken an evening hack with Janet and without warning, Pudding jumped in the air, spooked by an odd shaped plant. I mentioned before that I have come off three times, well this was the third. I was on the ground before I knew it, unhurt, and with no memory of falling. It was obvious that I needed to address this; I had seen YouTube clips of riders who remain seated whilst their horse performed aerial gymnastics, so what was their secret?

I had always taken lessons with Jonny, but he moved on to his own yard miles away. His place had been taken by Karen, a serious eventer with an encyclopaedic knowledge of horses. I shared my concerns with her and she kindly agreed to give me ad hoc lessons.

"Let's begin by just watching you ride" she said, so she stood eyes fixed on me while I circled the ménage around her.
"You need to change your seat position."

She talked me through a simple adjustment to the way I sat in the saddle. I was to push my pelvis forward and sit back on my seat bones. My legs needed to stay off the horse while he was moving (instead of my usual habit of clamping on for dear life whenever we went faster than a trot) and shorten my reins. We practised the trot using my newfound skills and to my surprise, Pudding began to speed up and trot with pace and determination.

"You are letting him move now, you were putting too much pressure on the wrong places before and restricting his gait," she said.

Wow. During the following weeks I practiced this new position and to my utter amazement, sat through a few spooks with no problem. It felt like I had been given the keys to the treasure chest, this was powerful stuff. Whilst I am touching a very large piece of wood while saying this, I have not fallen off or come close to falling off since that day. Which was just as well, as I had something big in mind. I have often found myself looking at the Sports Endurance website and pawing the screen at the exciting possibilities presented. One in particular jumped out at me, Catton Hall. This was a ten-mile route through the halls private estate, only made available to the sports endurance riders. It looked glorious.

After what felt like the longest wait ever, the morning of the Catton Park ride was upon me. Ruth had made arrangements, so she could come and was bringing Janet's mare, as her horse was being entertained by her daughter. We were both a bubble of excitement when we set off and thankfully it was Sunday morning and the roads were clear. As we drove into the field parking in glorious sunshine, we were greeted by trailers, horseboxes and some nifty little 'mini paddocks' constructed with plastic poles and tape. In the distance we could see riders at various points around the course, some moving at considerable pace; which was exactly what our horses fixated on as we unloaded them.

For two quite lazy cobs, the feel of grass underfoot put a real spring in the step and our request for a light trot up the first hill was translated by them to mean a full-on gallop to the top. Ruth kept repeating that her horse would be worn out after the first mile, several miles later and still full of life, we concluded that these horses had no intention of slowing down. They were having fun and determined to make the most of it.

Now if you had said to me that I would be galloping up hills, cantering across fields and dealing with a horse so light on his feet he was virtually doing the opening sequence of Riverdance, I would not have believed you. Yet there was something about the joy this horse was feeling that worked its magic on me. I was going with the flow and loving it. At one point, we were galloping up a hill while I was trying to turn my Camcorder on – words I never thought you would hear me say. My newly learnt position in the saddle was very empowering!

One of the real pleasures of the Catton ride is the fact that it is virtually all off road. Field after field presented itself to us, with a defined route carefully mown the day before. We circled round fields of barley, peas, hay and a couple of crops which neither Ruth or I could identify. We watched buzzards soar in the air, fluffy clouds scud across the sky, enjoyed the refreshing breeze on top of the hills and the panoramic view across the patchwork landscape below us. Every now and again one us would suggest we had a canter and the other would quickly second the motion; and before we knew it we were bouncing along and having fun.

What a buzz at Catton

We were a couple of hours in when our route took us through a farm and past some other riders when Ruth asked

"Do you have any idea how many miles we have done so far?"
"Six and half" was the very precise reply.

Neither of us could believe we had covered so much ground so quickly. The last time we did a ten-mile hack it took around five hours, although we did have a pub stop. We decided this would be a good place to a break, have something to eat, and let the horses have a brief rest. Pudding had no problem embracing the moment and dived headlong into the long grass. Ruth's mare just stood there with her eyes virtually shut.

"My god, I've killed her" said Ruth staring at the mare with a look of alarm.

At this point she pulled the sandwiches she had prepared out of her bum bag. I have never seen such sorry looking specimens in all my life. As she cupped the two crumbled pieces of bread in her hand we laughed, apparently the butter had been so cold it wouldn't spread when she had rushed to make them that morning and they had since spent several hours squashed in a bum bag.

"There is no way I would consider eating this normally, but today I am so hungry I'll eat anything" she remarked with a mouthful of bread.

I had brought two Fudge bars to share, with the chocolate coating having melted in the heat, we resorted to sucking them out of the wrapper. Rest over and with our faces covered in chocolate, we used a couple of hay bales as mounting blocks and began the onward journey. We need not have been concerned about Ruth's mare, she sprung back into life and continued on her way with renewed vigour.

We were doubling back on ourselves at this final stage of the ride and I can honestly say I did not want it to end. We squeezed in one last gallop and then let the horses stretch their necks before turning into the field parking and back to the van. To our absolute delight, catering had arrived, so after we had sorted our horses we hot-footed it to their van. Two freezing cold cans of Vimto later, we were about as happy as it comes. We had no idea at this point that the main A road we needed to get home had been closed for the afternoon and we would soon be spending a couple of hours re-routed over winding hills and vales to get home.

Chapter Seven

Catton was a shot of pure excitement and left us wanting more. As I sat half watching television and half playing on my phone, a string of messages started to flow between Ruth, Janet and I that finished with us agreeing we would book a riding holiday immediately. Ruth leapt into action and within an hour had found a brilliant proposition, a hall in the peak district who operated a bed and breakfast, allowed you to take your own horse and provided maps for a wide range of local hacks. By the end of the week it was booked.

As it got closer Janet found she could not get the time away from work, which felt like such a shame, but we completely understood. Ruth and I spent the week before engrossed in preparation. We had some calculations to make, factoring two horses in a van with just over a tonne payload, we really didn't have that much more weight allowance to play with. Obviously, we were going to take tipples, and snacks, and crisps, but they were clearly essentials. I announced that for everything else we should pack light and try to keep it limited to one small backpack.

Finally, it was the morning of our holiday and we were both at the yard just after seven, not having slept a wink the night before with excitement. We took the various bits and bobs from our cars and stowed them in the van, loaded the horses and got going. The sat nav was programmed for Rushop Hall, it had calculated the route and as I didn't have a clue where it was, we were going to follow the arrow until arrived. Now this place is in the centre of the peak district and there really isn't any way of getting there without negotiating steep windy hills. While Ruth chatted merrily in the seat next to me, I was experiencing hot sweats as I punched the accelerator trying to get us up the virtually vertical hill climbs, then work a clutch/brake combo to stop us hurtling off the edge as we descended on the other side through one set after another of hairpin bends. I was not enjoying the fact that we had to travel down huge stretches of windy road where only a flimsy metal barrier separated us from thin air and a fall into some wooded abyss miles below us.

By the time I got to a long stretch of flat road there were that many cars behind us I simply couldn't see any end to them. I took the opportunity to pull into a layby to let them pass and give me a chance to loosen the vice like grip my hands had adopted on the steering wheel. To my great relief the worst of it was behind us and we eventually arrived at our destination just before lunch. We were immediately perplexed by the number of entrances, one said 'no car café' so we assumed that it couldn't be that one and gently moved forward to the next. It seemed to stop suddenly so that one didn't make sense either.

"Don't worry" said Ruth disappearing the through the cab door "I'll go and find out".

A few minutes later she returned and said that we had overshot and it was the first entrance we needed. I really did not fancy reversing when it involved an uphill climb on a narrow lane, so we decided to take the owners advice and drive to the end, turn around and come back. I had begun to relax thinking that the demands on my driving were almost at an end, but sadly that was not the case. The end of the lane was on a steep hill, although it had a wide entrance, the road we were meant to be turning around on was relatively narrow. The hot sweat returned as I moved forward and taking as wide a circle as I possibly could, began to turn. Slowly we nudged forward, and the van began to lean uncomfortably to one side; I was absolutely petrified that it would topple over. A few feet more and we were now turning on a 1:3 gradient with the van lurching even more to the right. At this point I was dripping in sweat and in the middle of a mild panic attack. A few more feet, then a few more and we were finally turned and facing down the hill to the lane we had just come from. After taking a moment to gather myself, we crept along the track and back to the right entrance.

I now took a proper look at where I had to drive. It was a very tight turn on a narrow driveway with yet another drop down. My heartrate still hadn't found its regular pace from the last tight turn, so I felt I had already been to the briefing room, received instructions and was primed and ready to get on with my next panic attack and full dousing down. We began the turn and again the van began to lean to the right, just a little, then a bit more. Slowly we inched on until we had eventually made the turn and were easing our way down the driveway, past the house and the 'no car café' and round to a circular section of tarmac on which we could park.

Getting settled

The owner, Liz, was there to greet us and as soon as we stopped Ruth jumped out and was chatting merrily. It took me a few minutes to gather myself together before I staggered out of the van and offered an extremely moist hand for a formal greeting. She was clean, tidy, very welcoming, a keen horsewoman and efficiency in action. She left after confirming our meal order and showing us where to place the horses, as we had decided we would come and get her when we were ready to see our rooms.

Already we knew that we were going to like the place, it was immaculate, with small outbuildings of local limestone which had been converted into holiday lets, dry stone walls, a line of stables and views across the moors. It was such a relief to have arrived in one piece and finally stretch my legs. The horses were making noises in the van, they were keen to get out and I am sure the journey hadn't been much fun for them either.

Pudding exited first and wanted to take a moment to breathe in the fresh Derbyshire air, then Ebony who did the same. We walked them over to a large grassed walkway which marked the entrance to their field, closed the gate and let them have a stretch. They had a trot around, a sniff and within minutes settled into eating the grass looking very content, while we sat on the bench eating our sandwiches watching them.

The tour of our rooms made Ruth and I look at each other with gleeful nods and smiles. We were on the first floor of the sizeable but homely Rushop Hall. We had our own lounge, with big leather sofas, a fire, television and big Georgian windows with views across the hills. Across the large landing from the lounge were our bedrooms. Ruth had a large room at the front of the house, tastefully decorated in cream and taupe with her own drinks table, TV and en-suite. I was thrilled with my room. It was equally as large, with duck egg walls, cream bedding, a big en-suite, my own drinks table and a view from the back of the house which allowed me to see the entrance to the field where our horses were.

We deposited our things in the rooms, have crept through the entrance hall hoping the bags with all our alcohol didn't clank too much as we passed the owners lounge door. We had decided before the trip that we would hack on every one of the three days we were there, so once everything was sorted Ruth was eager to get going. In no time at all we were tacked up and off down the driveway which had caused me so much distress on the way in.

Following the carefully laminated instructions provided by Liz, we embarked on our first adventure, a hack through the intriguingly named Sparrowpit. After a small section down a busy road, we turned past a row of quaint cottages and up the track past farms, dry stone walls with restless young bullocks which Pudding took some getting past, then alongside an otter sanctuary, on through lovely villages, a bridleway and the final stretch through a field which the instructions said we could 'canter if we chose to'. Both Ruth and I stopped, staring at the field, reviewing our options

"I wasn't expecting sheep" I said

"No, me neither" she replied

"It is uphill, but the sheep are spread all over the place, if we start cantering up there, won't some of them end up running in front of us?"

"Oh yes, they will. And what will the horses do?"

"God knows"

"Let's just walk" she said

"Yes, let's just walk"

So we did. We walked to the top of the hill, through the gate and completed the home stretch on a lovely sandy track which had panoramic views across the moors to the hills beyond.

By the time we had got the horses settled in the field we were ready for a drink and a rest. We made ourselves a cup of tea and sat in the lounge for a chat. With just over an hour to go before our meal, we both felt like a short nap and a shower, so we agreed to meet on the landing at five to seven.

Ruth was out first and gave a quick knock on the door

"Coming" I shouted as I opened the door to see her standing there in black pants and a t-shirt.

"Look at you – I thought you said we should pack light!" she said indigently.

Indeed, I had, in fact I had been quite firm on the subject. But my nerve went when I thought about the fact we were staying in a *hall* and imagined going down to dinner with white linen and full silver service in a pair of jogging pants. So I packed a cerise linen shift dress, matching necklace and a cream pashmina. I did have open toed sandals, but they proved completely impractical for getting across the yard, so I had to resort to wearing my yard boots instead.

"Honestly, I don't believe you" Ruth repeated

"I know, I'm sorry. I bottled"

We walked down the stairs, with her still chunnering and across the yard to the designated dining area. Opening the door, we stepped into a small flagged entrance with a big sign asking us to remove our shoes, we obliged and opened the second door to the dining area. We were in fact eating in the café area. A large room with stone flagged floors, big chunky wooden tables and lots of interesting posters and plaques on the walls. Without a doubt Ruth was wearing exactly the right get-up and I looked like I was only there because my big date had stood me up.

Our hostess appeared in jeans and a gislet and cheerily announced that we were the only ones eating tonight, so we could sit wherever we liked. Pulling up our chairs we settled into our seafood risotto which was absolutely divine, followed by brownie and ice cream. A bottle of smooth red wine was well underway, and we felt altogether content with life. We decided to take a hot drink in our lounge and returned to our rooms via the field to check on the horses. It was such a thrill to have Pudding so close to hand, I loved the idea that I could check on him at any time. He seemed perfectly happy munching away and hardly looked up.

Once we were back in our lounge we started to decant the contents of our goody bags. 3 bottles of wine, two bottles of gin, multiple tins of tonic water, 2 huge bags of Sensations crisps, nuts, cookies, muffins, chocolate and cheesy biscuits. Yes, that would do nicely. Two drinks and a bag of crisps later we realised that the events of the day had totally worn us out, so at the incredibly early time of nine thirty we both turned in and were asleep within minutes.

The following morning, after a glorious night's sleep, I woke to the sound of sheep and a something I could not quite identify. I got out of bed and had a look through the window, there was a mist across the fields and hills beyond; it looked like someone from special effects had been up all night with a smoke machine. I put my reading glasses on and with blurry vision peered towards the field, I thought I could just make out the shape of the horses near the gate, so I grabbed my phone, took a picture and sent it to Janet.

After a reviving cup of tea, I negotiated the shower for the second time. It was only now that I realised that not only did my en-suite not have a blind, but that the window was perfectly visible to anyone on the drive below. A fact that was brought home as two hikers strode past acknowledging me as they went. I spent the next fifteen minutes washing whilst crawling under the window whenever I needed to pass it.

Back in the café we were famished and ready for breakfast. The husband, donned in a pinny came and took our cooked breakfast order; we both opted for 'the works' and while that was being cooked we helped ourselves to some thick and creamy yoghurt with freshly made stewed rhubarb. Yummy.

"this is sooo good" said Ruth

"I'll say" I replied.

One cooked breakfast and a pot of tea later we were ready for the off. We grabbed the horses, tied them to the hitching points on the van and began to tack up. Within a few minutes I was aware of a lady with a small dog stood by the wall just watching us

"Good morning" she said cheerily

"Good morning"

"I love horses" she observed

"Oh, do you, do you have one of your own? I enquired

"No, I just love them"

After a little more discourse she knew the names of our horses and had given them both a stroke.

"I'm here on a walking holiday" she continued "but I don't really walk"

I couldn't help but look down to see her boots were immaculate. I wondered about liking the idea of something, but not actually the reality of it. The reality is usually a world away from the dream, it's hard work, un-sanitised and full of things you had not imagined or anticipated. I am glad for the gilded dream, I am not sure we would get into half the things we do if we had any real idea of what was actually ahead of us. And we would miss amazing the experience it affords.

Not quite sure how best to reply simply said "well, have a good day then".

We mounted and just as we were turning to go down the drive I heard the sound again, then again, then again. What on earth was it? It was like a high-pitched whine, then suddenly the culprit came into view, a small hairy pony in the end stable. He was so small you could just see his ears and a huge tuft of forelock over the stable door, but what he lacked in height he made up for in noise. He had clearly been practising his act, should film or TV ever call, as he could do little jumps on the spot allowing you to get a split-second view of his eyes and poofball forelock. Working the whinny and the jump together it was a killer comedy combo. We were utterly enamoured with Whinny the Whiner.

Leaving him behind we made off down the driveway, up the lane and across the A road to the bridle path. We had decided that we wanted to hack to Edale, so Liz provided us with another laminated route map and it all seemed pretty straight forward. The bridlepath would take us most of the way and then all we had to do was catch the road down into Edale. We went through the first gate onto a sandy track and then through the second gate onto the main path in the direction of Mam Tor. What greeted us stopped us both in our tracks.

"How can this possibly be a bridleway?" gasped Ruth

"You've got to be kidding me" I said staring at what lay ahead.

How anything was supposed to make its way along there was a complete mystery. We stared in horror at the gorge, with grassy banks either side and the floor covered in boulders. Little one, great big ones, sharp ones; all randomly dumped in one unrelenting uneven motorway of stone.

Nothing for miles

"How is a horse supposed to walk on that?" continued Ruth "surely their hooves will slip through the gaps and get stuck . It could permanently damage their tendons"

After much debate we resolved to try and give it a go, but after a few steps we felt the whole thing was an accident waiting to happen, so we stopped, pretty much stuck where we were.

"dear god, this is horrendous" I gasped.

After another review of the situation we decided to try and get onto the bank and follow the thin track left by walkers and cyclists. We dismounted, grabbed the reins and with Pudding and I going first we climbed up the side and teetered long the mile-long shelf of grass until we reached the next gate. Once through there was a wide sandy circle from which two bridle paths made their departure. Both ran as far as the eye could see, laid with the same boulders as the path we had just left. By now we were feeling pretty frazzled, so we resolved to turn around, pick our way carefully along the grassy banks we had just travelled down and hack on the road.

After miles of busy A road, with lorries and cars flying past us we finally got to the turn and began our ascent up towards Mam Tor. Once at the top we could see the point at which the bridlepath joined the road and felt another sense of frustration at whichever council numpty had sanctioned several hundred tonnes of rock to be dropped on an otherwise beautiful cross-country path.

Much to our delight the road was closed to motorists as it had been newly laid, and they were undergoing 'sweeping'. We began our descent enjoying the sunshine, the glorious views and a small drama every ten minutes when the road sweeper decided to make yet another drive past.

Eventually we reached the flat of the valley and after a small trek past a few farms and B&Bs arrived in Edale and a very welcome stop at the pub Ruth knew. We turned the horses into the drive and past the rows of gleaming Morgens that were being admired by the various members of the Morgen car society that had gathered there that day. After a quick enquiry, we were assured that horses were welcome, so we parked ourselves on the grass and dismounted.

Pudding was over the moon, there was a great expansive lawn to go at and he took no time at all in getting on with it. I decided he wasn't going to go anywhere, so I tied his reins up and left him to it. Ruth was less carefree, she was worried Ebony might lean on one of the expensive cars, so she opted to sit on the bench holding the reins and let the mare eat her way around her. After a quick trip to the bar we sat just enjoying a drink in the sunshine.

"Are those Shires?" came a man's voice from nowhere.
We looked round to see a small wiry chap, with a lived in face, sat back on a chair pipe in hand "I say, are those Shires?"

"No, actually they're cobs" replied Ruth "but they do look a bit like Shires, only smaller"

"Ahh" said the man, leaning even further back in his chair. He took a whiff of his pipe "my mother hated Shires. My father had two, but they used to chase her out of the field whenever she went in". He chuckled quietly to himself at the memory.

We sat chatting for a few moments and it transpired that he originated from an area not far from where we lived and knew it well. We then spent a few more minutes confirming whether this building or that was still standing as he drew on his pipe, often taking a sharp gasp when we told him his school was now an MOT centre or the cinema was a fitness club.

After a very pleasant hour we said out goodbyes and narrowly missing one of the cars we turned the corner. Ruth leaned over

"Did you catch the smell?' she grinned and with a wink said, "that was not tobacco he was smoking".

We left the pub and circled down towards a small cabin selling handmade ice-creams. The assistant behind the counter was over the moon to see horses, she told us not to dismount and quickly brought thick creamy strawberry ice creams for us and a couple of carrots for the horses. We were surprised to learn that within a few minutes we had managed to find another person who originated from Cheshire and was keen to catch up. We chatted in the sunshine for a while and then turned for home.

It took us no time at all to get to the top of Mam Tor, the horses were eager to get back and to be honest, so were we. We had set off at ten that morning and it was now nearing four in the afternoon; both of us had stepped beyond the comfort point, legs were aching, and feet were numb. Once on the main A road we trudged on and on and on – I am sure they had extended the thing while we were gone. When we came to the point on the road that was level with the hall Pudding stopped dead. He knew that we should be turning and kept bending his neck and virtually nodding at me 'it's there lady, come on, look!' You didn't need to be a horse whisperer to know exactly what was going on in that pony's head. When I nudged him on, he grudgingly took steps forward whilst still nodding at the hall as we passed. The lane for home was a heart-breaking quarter of a mile away and Pudding who was leading had dropped down to a snail's pace. By the time we turned the corner both my legs were numb, so I decided to jump off and walk with him until we got to the hall. I have to admit, it took a few minutes before the circulation returned and I could actually walk anywhere; but eventually we arrived at the driveway and turned two exhausted horses out into the field.

Ruth and I could hardly speak

"I am absolutely shattered" I mumbled "seriously, my legs are numb"

"Me too. Let's just have a nap for a bit" she replied

"Best suggestion ever" I agreed

Later that evening whilst at dinner, reprising our pants and dress combo, we spoke to Liz about the rocky bridleway

"Oh yes" she nodded "there was quite an uproar when it first went down. We always use the grassy path at the side"

Ruth and I just looked at each other aghast.

"I did wonder why you were hacking down the main road" she said as she departed for the kitchen

"Grassy path at the side" I whispered when she was out of earshot "grassy path at the side! She could have mentioned it earlier"

Liz returned with our main course, put it down and enquired after her laminated map

"Sorry" said Ruth " I must have dropped it somewhere"
"Do you have any idea where? " inquired Liz, looking rather alarmed at this sudden turn of events
"I'm not sure" said Ruth coyly
"Well, can you remember the last time you had it?" Liz continued
"I think it was probably at the beginning when we were going through the gates" replied Ruth
"Mmm. I shall go out and have a look for it later" muttered Liz turning again for the kitchen
"Crickey, I thought she had loads of them. I didn't realise it was her only one" said Ruth quietly
"I think we're in the doghouse now" I replied smiling.

After our meal we wandered over to the field to have a look at the horses and check they were OK. I climbed onto the gate to get a better view and shouted across to Pudding 'hiya baby, how you doing?' He looked up briefly, acknowledged me, then continued eating.

"He's OK" I said to Ruth climbing down from the gate. We walked back to the house with me shimmying along in my cerise number, pashmina wrapped around my shoulders and yard boots on my feet

"god you look ridiculous" said Ruth.

That evening we stayed in our lounge, sprawled across our settees, drinking G&Ts, eating snacks and generally having a good giggle. Around eleven o'clock we turned in and for the second night running I was asleep in seconds.

The following morning, I awoke and tried to turn over, then the pain hit me. I ached from head to toe – arms, legs, lower back, the works. I lay there contemplating my throbbing limbs with the distant sound of Whinny the Whiner in my ear. It took about ten minutes to get out of bed and stagger over to my kettle to make a cup of tea; the average arthritic ninety-year-old is on better form than I was that morning. Tea consumed I felt refreshed enough to have a stab at a shower and creaked my way into the en-suite, only to emerge from the shower ten minutes later, see two hikers walk past and instinctively go to duck under the window. I got stuck half way and only ended up thrusting my chest towards the window, trying to hide my modesty with a small flannel while nodding good morning to the rather bewildered couple below.

I met Ruth on the landing and she looked as battered as me. Both of us were bowed legged and staggered to the stairs looking as though we were carrying two large invisible balls between our legs. As we turned on the stairs the smell began to permeate our nostrils

"What is that smell" asked Ruth "it was there yesterday as well"

On closer inspection it turned out be my boots. I felt for Liz, I really did. In two days we had lost her map and stunk her house out.

At breakfast we opted for the same as yesterday and soon got stuck in. Liz enquired whether we wanted any more details of the Pennine trail she had told us about when we arrived. This had been greeted by great excitement when we first heard the story of how she and her friends had spent sixteen days riding over a hundred miles across the Pennines, staying over-night at farms and pubs along the way. Our excitement was somewhat diminished today, as we had only ridden for two days and we were already broken women.

Hello neighbour

"I think we will need a bit more time before we tackle that one" we responded flatly.

Outside the morning had its trademark mists and the brooding moors which made us feel as though we had been dropped into a Wuthering Heights film set. It had a very rugged and chiselled charm which made it so unmistakably Derbyshire. We agreed that we were not up to much, so settled on the two-hour Sparrowpit hack we had done on the first day. We eventually set off down the driveway at the slowest speed we had ever hacked, neither man or beast was in any hurry this morning; slow and steady was the only way it was going down today.

During the first part of the hack the muscles began to relax a little and we plodded on enjoying the beauty of our surroundings; but as we turned on the final stretch for home we both felt ready to get off and imagined what it would be like to get into a relaxing hot bath, obviously with a nice cup of tea.

We reached canter field knowing that we were about fifteen minutes away and came to an abrupt halt. The sheep had gone and in their place was a herd of large hairy bulls.

"you've got to be kidding me" I gasped in horror

Ruth was incensed "why the hell would you put bulls in a field that horses have right of way through"

We sat there trying to figure out if there was any way at all we could get through the field, while both horses fixated on the bulls ahead of them, quietly snorting.

"It's just not going to happen" said Ruth "they are stood right by the gate"
I just wanted to cry "are we going to have to turn back?"
"Looks like it" said an equally dejected Ruth.

We turned around and began to retrace our steps, both feeling pretty desperate to find some sort of shortcut back to the hall.

I remembered a track which spurred off in that direction, which wasn't far from where we were.

"I am sure there is a sign" I said, spirits beginning to rise
"But what if we can only get so far and then have to turn back?" sighed Ruth.

We agreed that we would ask the next person we saw and within moments a farmer came trundling along in his land rover

"Oh no" he replied in answer to our question "that path is for walkers only. There's a gate at the end that you couldn't get your horses through"

In unison both of us sank in our saddles

"Why don't you use the bridlepath at the end of the lane" he continued "that's the best route"
"Because someone has stuck a herd of bulls in there" I said indignantly, now beginning to suspect it was probably him.
"Your horses not good with cows then?" he said, putting his car in gear and pulling away
"Is any horse?" I shouted after him.

So, we back tracked through lanes, tracks and paths until we reached the intersection with the main road. A cunning plan began to develop; rather than cross over and take the scenic detour, let's just hack down the main road and get back in a fraction of the time. So that's what we did. Several miles in and climbing up another hill, I longed for a lovely flat route

"Next time we are taking our break in Norfolk" I shouted back to Ruth.

Our exhausted ponies plodded on and on, looking more and more like a Donkey Sanctuary advert. Eventually we turned into the driveway and down to the courtyard. This had been the hack to end all hacks, our little party was totally spent. Liz appeared to check we were OK and mentioned that she was surprised to see us hacking down the A road again.

"She must think we're mental" I said to Ruth after she had departed "miles and miles of glorious countryside and we are always on the main road"

The drive home seemed to take forever. I had tried to make a detour to avoid the steep hills and hair pin bends but ended up right back at the point they started, so with gritted teeth and white knuckles, we bobbed up and down until eventually we were through and back to the yard. The horses were delighted to be back, and both fell asleep within minutes of being walked in their stables. We said our goodbyes, agreed to clear out the van the following day and made our way home. It had been quite an adventure and probably not quite what we had envisioned, but huge fun all the same.

The following day I met Janet at the yard

"Thanks for the picture" she said, "but where were the horses?"

I opened the phone and stared at the picture. I had sent her a photo of the field with the distant outline of a boulder and a water trough.

Chapter Eight

To set the scene, when Phil asked me what I would like for a birthday present, it was a no-brainer – a set of horse clippers. I have a Highland pony, who left to his own devices looks like a woolly mammoth. He needed clipping, especially as Autumn approached as he would double in size with the amount of layering, which was very uncomfortable for him when he got hot and sweaty. On the last two occasions Jonny had clipped him for me. We had walked Pudding over to Jonny's stables, where in a blizzard of white hair Jonny worked his way around this little pony, occasionally pausing to catch his breath. The stable floor was covered in hair and Jonny had to wade through furrows of the stuff to attack from different angles

"It's like clipping the abominable snowman" he declared.

Pudding never flinched, he had been clipped several times a year by his previous owner, so he really could not give two hoots about it. This helped me make up my mind, rather than spending money for someone else to do it, I would get a pair of clippers and do it myself. After four clips I would have recouped the cost of the clippers anyway.

So here I was with a pair of Masterclip Hunter clippers and no clue where to start. I sought help from YouTube and found plenty of footage of people demonstrating how easy clipping was; you start at the neck and basically run the clippers in the opposite direction to the hair. How hard can that be?

After the morning's rush of people had gone, I secured Pudding in his stable and nervously began. I ran the clippers up his neck and stood back. He was not remotely bothered, and I had a lovely straight line of clipped hair. Well that was straight forward enough, so off I went, this way and that to the gentle burr of the clippers. I would routinely stop to check they were not too hot, spray them with coolant, then continue. I had been at it for over an hour and finally completed the body, so I stood back to admire my work. Whilst it looked fine when I was close up, I was not prepared for what I was about to see. My jaw dropped at the full horror of the view before me – he looked like an aerial shot of a ploughed field.

The yard owner passed at that moment, took one look and burst out laughing

"How's it going?" she enquired

"Not too well" I replied.

"Good for you for giving it a go. You're braver than me" she smiled as she left.

Brave was not the word I would have used. Panic set in and I went off in search of help which I quickly found in the shape of Judy, a lady who had recently joined the yard and had a history of showing horses. She stepped into the stable and did not seem in any way as alarmed as me on the sight before her. Holding the clippers, she pulled Puddings skin taut and ran the clippers over a small area. To my huge relief, she had clipped all the hair in that area to the same length. She repeated the same move a couple of times then handed the clippers back to me, so I could try. I cannot tell you how happy I was to see how good it was now looking. Gone was the field and in its place a lovely smooth and even coat.

I was still terrified of doing the face, or the legs for that matter. Judy stepped in and completed them for me. What a lifesaver!

We were now at lunchtime, it had quite literally taken all morning. But I could step back and observe my pony with an air of pride, you could actually see his shape and he looked lovely.

To double my delight, he obviously needed extra rugs. I got to play with my rug collection whilst deciding which would be the most suitable combination for this occasion. As I might have mentioned before, he is never knowingly under-rugged.

Clipping Pudding was not the only new thing for me that month. My daughter and I had attended a Neuro Linguistics Programming taster weekend in London some months before and we decided that we would like to go back and complete a course to become practitioners. As with all dates in the diary, they seem to be a lifetime away when you jot them down, but in a heartbeat, they are right upon you. The plan was a simple one, I would go down to London on the Sunday night, stay with her and her housemates at their house and return home at the end of the course.

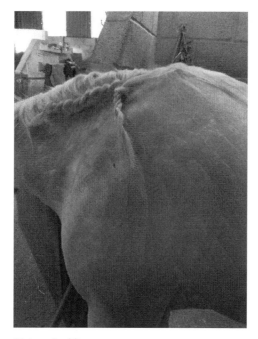

Stripey Pudding

The train journey down seemed so familiar. For the last year of my job, I would routinely travel down to London two or three times a week. Catching the red eye at seven am, so I would be in the capital and at my meeting destination for nine. I really do not mind early starts and always enjoyed the buzz of work; my role was frontline business to business. It was enormous fun and I loved it. Sitting on that train nearly two years on, I could remember exactly what I used to; how I would be preparing for my meeting and how I used to feel, almost as though it were yesterday.

Walking through the main concourse at Euston I could see that little had changed. There was always a sea of people craning their necks to read the timetables on the electric boards above them. Suddenly a board would flicker, and a platform number would appear next to a specific train; it looked like a starting pistol had just fired, as dozen people would grab their bag and start running, darting past others in an attempt to be one of the first on the train to secure a seat.

I approached the escalator and descended into the bowels of the station, the ever packed underground. Swiped my card and descended even further to the platforms below. The air was stale and hot, with the odd rush of breeze as the train approached with a whirr and a small thread of exhaust hit the nostrils. For nearly an hour I swayed in my seat as the train thundered from one stop to the next, until I finally reached mine. As I walked down the platform dragging my case, I was praying that this was a station with an escalator and not one with a thousand stairs.

Once I was safely inside the house, with a cup of tea in hand, it was time to catch up with everyone. I had not seen Sia for months, so it was fun to regal stories of Pudding and all our adventures. But it was a big day tomorrow, I had not really had to use my brain for quite a while, so I fully expected that it would be a stretch to spend a week doing an intensive training course. With that in mind, I retired to bed with the alarm set for stupid o'clock.

The morning was still a rush, as I was the last one in the bathroom the hot water had gone, so I had a short and enlivening cold shower. Quick breakfast and a power walk with my daughter to the underground, emerging like rabbits from a burrow twenty minutes later at Tower Hill. We entered our conference hotel, registered and spent a good few minutes trying to decide which of the many rows of seats we were going to sit in. Too close to the front and you could get picked on, which was dangerous as we had only scan read our pre-course work. Too far to the back and we couldn't see anything. We opted for the safety of the middle.

The course got underway and we both relaxed, our host was easy to listen to and proved entertaining as well as educational. It was fascinating to learn how the brain takes in information and processes it. To understand the power of language. And mesmerising to watch the diagrams showing which way the eyes look depending on the information they are retrieving.

After the lunch break we were going to practice our first learns in small groups of three. The exercise involved working through any bad feeling or emotions you may be holding against someone else that was directly affecting your relationship with them. My little group had an immediate volunteer, a slight Swedish lady who was struggling in the relationship with her step daughter. The other group member, an older male decided that he was definitely cut out for the role of observer/note taker, which left me as the lead/questioner. I felt pretty positive if I did look down at my hand, I would see it was holding the short straw.

We began quite easily with the first section, 'Self', allowing her to talk freely about how she was feeling and what her view of the current situation was. The next exercise called 'Other' involved her putting herself in her daughters' shoes and telling us what she imagined that was like, how the daughter was thinking and feeling. The very last exercise 'Meta Position' was one designed to bring closure; as she became the third person, the arbitrator who had to give guidance to herself.

So far everything had gone really well, and I had managed to use most of the questions we had been given as guidance without spending too long looking at my notes. But this last section suddenly became tricky. I asked if she could 'see' what she needed to do next or could she visualise the next steps. She suddenly became quite disturbed, no she couldn't see anything however hard she tried. I was beginning to get worried, this was not going well. Then from nowhere I must have remembered something said earlier in the day and asked her to 'imagine' the next steps. To my utter relief she relaxed and proceeded to talk about her ideas.

After the exercise was completed we sat chatting about our session and what she told me was an absolute revelation. I had spent my whole life quite easily being able to visualise things – it presented no problem at all for me to play any desired outcomes in mind, as though I was watching the television. Yet here was a lovely young lady telling me that she simply couldn't 'see' anything. Her brain processed and relayed information in a completely different way. It did bring home the fact that we are all so very different, our experiences and responses are unique to us so the way we handle the things that happen, has to be unique to us. There are models we can follow to deal with our mind-sets, but ultimately, we cannot truly know how another person perceives their world.

As we took our first afternoon break my daughter joined me looking almost ashen. Her group had been quite a shocker. Like me she had ended up conducting the exercise, but her volunteer was a young girl who had been abused by her father, run away from home, got involved with drugs and then been battered by her boyfriend.

"Honestly mum" she whispered "I didn't know where to start"
"Are you OK" I asked, now concerned that she was being exposed to things that she was not prepared for.
"Yeah, yeah, I'm fine. I just wasn't expecting it"

We began bright and early the following morning with some more gems, one which I particularly liked as it dealt with Self Limiting Beliefs. The voice in your head that says you cannot do something. Everyone else may be able to do, in fact it is probably quite easy for them. But not for you.

My goodness, how you tackle this is a book in itself. We practised 'timeline' techniques, dealing with particular points in an individual's history when they first accepted the belief that they could not do a particular thing. There were exercises which involved us taking our volunteer on a mental journey back to those points when they accepted what others had said so we could now begin to address it.
We also looked at what we would like to achieve and what we would need to do to get there. Learning the importance of language and how the brain will fix on our words, so it is better saying "I will be fit and healthy" rather than "I don't want to be fat and unfit". So, we don't work away from negatives but work towards positives.

We undertook more exercises and as the days rolled by, we were all feeling relaxed in each other's company, open to sharing our own stories and emotions. The final day was to finish with us each doing a presentation to the rest of the group. Now I know my daughter hates presenting with a passion, she gets overcome with nerves and feels physically sick. But I was amazed at how she adopted the techniques she had learned and rocked it. I could not have been any prouder.

As we walked back to the house I asked her how the morning session had gone, as I knew she was again the lead in an exercise dealing with issues which were holding people back.

"Oh, I had someone who was abused as a child, one interfered with by their Imam and another struggling with alcohol"
"Really? Are you feeling alright?" I gasped
"honestly, water off a ducks' back now Mum" she smiled.

Over a cup of tea, I reflected on the correlation between our learning on the course and the Calm Rider Calm Horse material I had glanced at the week before. Could there actually be a connection between our mental beliefs and the way our horse responds to us. It was only a few months later when I was talking to a TREC course leader that she actually verbalised what I was suspecting. Horses pick up on everything, so being calm and focussed on your outcome will get you there a lot faster.

I find that incredible. And liberating. We are not bound or chained by anything that has happened in the past. We can start each fresh day with a fresh outlook and enjoy the rewards.

Phil had come down on the train for the final evening and decided to take the family to see a West End show to celebrate the end of our intensive week of training. We settled into our seats to watch the scary Woman in Black and around two hours later I felt Phil gently shaking my arm to wake me up

"Well done my dear, you slept through the whole lot'.

Chapter Nine

"Let's go to Kelsall" I said to Janet while we were busy mucking out. Her stable was opposite mine and it was possible to have a conversation while we were busy doing our jobs.

"Oh, I don't know" she said "I'd be a bit scared"

"We can take it nice and slow and only go at the speed you feel comfortable with" I assured her.

"Yes, alright then" she resolved "but I am only cantering when there is a hill"

The following weekend in a bubble of excitement we set off in the van to make the forty-minute journey. Kelsall is a farm ride, not as polished as Somerford, but set in glorious countryside with an optional purpose built all-weather strip in the centre appropriately called The Gallops. Janet had been out the night before at a birthday party and felt a little worse for wear, so we made a short stop at a petrol station to get a coffee.

"Ooo, I think I need one of those as well" she said eyeing the flapjacks. She had a particular penchant for a well-made flapjack.

I settled for a Danish custard and once purchased we sat in the van devouring our coffee and cakes

"that was so good" said Janet "I feel human again now".

A short while later we were turning into Kelsall, along the concrete drive, past the reception cabin and into the field parking. There was some sort of event taking place in the main jumping arena, so the parking area was pretty full. We jumped out and went to pay

"Will you be doing The Gallops today" enquired the assistant

"I'm not sure, maybe" I said

"Well you need to pay now if you are" she returned

"What would happen if we paid and then decided that we didn't want to do it?" I enquired

"You need to pay in advance if you are thinking of doing it" she replied

We could see this was going to be one of those circular conversations that would always end up with us back at the same point – pay for it now.

"Well then let's not" said Janet.

Feeling quite happy we had made the right decision we unloaded the horses and I noticed for the second time Pudding had bite marks on his neck where Ebony had bitten him, this time drawing blood. She was a mare, probably in season, so it was relatively normal behaviour between horses; but no fun for Pudding all the same. She had made an attempt at his neck on the trip back from our weekend away but this time it was worse, so I resolved to think of a solution before our next outing.

Heading off along the grassy track both horses were very excited to be out, and we spent the first section of the ride being jogged along by two ponies who were ready to let rip.

"I am not going fast" she repeated "And I will only canter when there's a hill"

We arrived at a wooded area, with a glorious canopy of trees, ferns and ponds to enjoy. We did a little trot and exited onto a grassy track which stretched as far as the eye could see.

"I might try a little canter" said Janet "is that OK?"
"Sure is" I replied

In one moment we were next to each other, the next she was almost a dot in the distance.
Feeling suddenly quite worried she would be in a state Pudding and I chased after, expecting her to find her completely shook up. Instead she was grinning from ear to ear and totally energised. We continued on our way with Janet declaring every small undulation 'a hill' and bombing off. I had thought Pudding could move, but Ebony on full flight was an absolute rocket. It was little wonder she had earned herself the nickname 'The Black Blur'.

At the end of the grassy track was a turning onto the second half of the ride, with lots of real hills. We walked to the bottom of the first one, signalled to go and the horses began to race each other to the top. I could feel Pudding surging forwards with Ebony in his eye line, determined to get past her and he was still bouncing around once we got to the top ready to go again. Janet and I were experiencing that euphoria that comes with an absolute adrenaline rush

"That was absolutely amazing" she said

"I am totally buzzing" I replied "I hope the headcam is working, wouldn't it be brilliant if we had got that on film"

"Please let it be working" she replied.

I had my doubts, it had been playing up and once or twice I had thought I'd captured a ride on film, only to get home and find nothing had recorded. I had checked it just after we started today, and it had looked pretty dead, so I wasn't holding out much hope.

We did one more canter that day and then followed the circuit back to the entrance point and our van. Full of energy and high as kites we made our way back, resolving to do it again as soon as possible.

Once I was back at home I decided to check and see if there was anything recorded. I sat there dumbfounded as the screen opened up before me and I was reliving the breath-taking race to the top of the hill. I messaged Janet and she was desperate to see it. After a small piece of editing I put a complication of our 'fast' bits together and popped them on YouTube. Within an hour we were up to forty views, but I suspect that was mainly me and Janet.

"I showed everyone at work" she grinned as we met the following day at the yard "they couldn't believe it was me, I was going *that* fast".

Indeed, she had been. And for the following week whenever we were out and there was even the smallest rise in the ground level, we would declare 'it's a hill'.

It would probably have been only a few weeks later when Janet decided to book a day off work, so we could do the Kelsall ride again. It had been so much fun and such an adrenaline rush that we longed to get back in the saddle and have a razz. I had been a little concerned that I found the gallop very bouncy and unless we were going uphill it was not that easy to ride. Once we were there and bobbing down the grassy track Janet told me that the best way to ride was to sit up out of the saddle. I resolved that I should give it a go.

Once out of the wood we tried to get our first canter, but the horses refused to do anything more than a trot. It had been raining heavily for days before and ground was deep underfoot, so with heavy hearts we decided that we wouldn't risk injury and just see how we went. However, everything changed when we got to the hill. On the second half of the ride the ground had a sandy composition and drained well, it was firm enough to canter on and the horses felt ready to give it a go. We hurtled up the hill and experienced the same burst of adrenaline as last time. We cantered along the field and I tried sitting up out of the saddle, Pudding shifted into another gear and revved up into full gallop. We were going at a lightening pace, but it was so easy to ride. I had my own epiphany – so this is how you do it.

Without really stopping we cantered and galloped around this section of the farm ride, with one glorious uphill gallop across the final field. High on excitement and emotion we dropped back to the grassy tack that led to the car park. Without doubt this had been the most exhilarating and enjoyable rides we had ever done. We relived the entire ride in the van home, obviously stopping for a congratulatory coffee and cake on the way.

I was very pleased that I had constructed a head partition using a shower curtain and bungees as we had arrived at Kelsall with no bite marks on Puddings' neck which was brilliant. Both of them had been fine with the partition in place, so it had seemed like a super cheap way of resolving the problem. After our return trip to the yard, I brought Pudding down the exit ramp and noticed a mark on his neck, how was this possible? I went back to the van for a closer look, peering in I could see the shower curtain with a bite sized hole in the centre, from which one black eye stared out. It looked quite menacing; like a scene from Psycho. No wonder Pudding had looked relieved to be out, he had been sharing stalls with Norman Bates.

When I finally got home I couldn't wait to see the footage. I opened the screen and it was blank. Bloody machine.

Now once you have had a taste of this exciting stuff, you want it again. It was obviously impractical to keep going back to the farm ride every weekend, so we looked for other places to have a little canter. One of our hacks around the Mere included a long stretch of grass, the very stretch on which Ruth and I had fallen off months earlier, but it did lend itself nicely for a little razz. We had decided to do exactly that and today we were being joined by a lovely young lady with a chestnut mare who was great when she was out with others, but this lovely mare did not like hacking on her own. I had talked with Grace many times and loved her positive outlook on life and her amazing sense of humour. She had a young son and could only get out on her horse when hubby was not working and able to look after him; so when she did get out and about it was an absolute joy.

We reached the strip of grass and let Janet set off first, I hung back for a moment then started in canter, sat up in my seat and Pudding then shot into gallop for the final bit.

"You were in front of me and then suddenly you were gone" gasped Grace as she caught up.
"We've been practising a gallop" I grinned.

We managed to sneak in a few more canters before we were finally back on the road and walking home.

"I really enjoyed that" said Grace
"Me too. Do you fancy going out this week?" I asked
"Let me ask the parents if they can sit and I will let you know" she replied.

That evening I got a text to say she had a pass for Tuesday morning so let's do it.

It was a glorious morning, as we set off on a hack which Grace knew had quite a few places for a little speed. We had a battle down the first section, a long tarmac driveway past a dairy farm. The horses could smell the cows and were not that enamoured with the idea that we were heading *towards* them. Once we were past the farm it became plain sailing, they happily trotted on until we reached out first gate. I leant forward to try and open it and my saddle slipped right round. I had one foot on the floor, the other in a stirrup and holding onto Pudding's mane for dear life. He just stood there with a very familiar 'the nutters at it again' expression on his face. Refusing to go down without a fight, I manoeuvred round and managed to dismount without any injury. After much fiddling we got the saddle back in position and the girth strap a hole higher on each side. When we were sure it was locked into position I found a fence to stand on and got back on.

"How does that feel?" enquired Grace

"Rock solid" I replied "so much better than before"

We made our way down the bridle path with Pudding and I leading the way, first in trot and then in canter. It was a lovely canter, just enough speed to be fun but not enough to get us into trouble. We approached the old wooden gate, I went to lift the handle and the whole thing, including the three feet of fence at either side, just fell to the ground.

"I didn't do anything" I exclaimed

We examined it to try and ascertain what had happened

"Look how rotten the wood is at the bottom" said Grace. Indeed, it was, the principle post had rotted the whole way through.

"Ah well, we've taken care of that alright. No one will be having any problems with that gate from now on" I grinned as we side stepped round it and continued on our way.

We motored on until eventually we turned into a track which led to a permissible field

"Honestly, you are allowed to ride in here" she said, looking at my disbelieving face.

It was hard to grasp that anyone was happy to let horses have a gallop anywhere, land was so precious with routes constantly being absorbed by builders; there were constant restrictions on being able to safely get out and about. I felt like shouting that to abusive motorists sometimes, when they were giving us a hard time about riding on the road. Show me where I can ride without having to go on a road and I will gladly take it. I have no more desire to be on a road than you have to see me there!

I viewed the field with mixed feelings, we would have to go around a blind corner in a moment and the field was covered in cow pats. I visualised turning the bend in full gallop, right into a herd of grazing cows.

"Let's just get around the corner first" I said "just to check there is nothing in here".

What lay before us was a glorious stretch of grass with nothing on it but us, with soaring heart I felt able to let rip, so after checking Grace was ready for the off, we thundered down that field in a flash. Pudding was jogging about when we got to the gate at the end, he had thoroughly enjoyed that and was ready to go again. Once through the gate we made our way to the bridle path that ran through the wood, with Pudding doing little jumps to get going. Once Grace was safely behind me, we set off again down the long stretch of track in full canter, just managing to pull to a stop when we reached the quite sudden end.

Out in the sunshine we hacked down a few lanes and circled around to the final bridle path for that day

"I think she'll go first now" said Grace looking at her mare "is your camera on? I'd love a video of me on her"

"I think so" I said "let's give it a go"

Grace moved her mare in front of Pudding and set off, within a heartbeat we were chasing after her. We managed to get our horses to slow to a trot as we passed a man walking his dog and then back to canter when we were safely passed.

"That was absolutely brilliant" declared Grace at the end

"I loved that" I replied, grinning for ear to ear.

We returned to the yard and I felt extremely fortunate to have had another truly amazing ride. I put Pudding in his stable and stood having a chat with him. He was such a good boy, always sensible and looking after me, even when I was doing acrobatics around him. A big hug and a couple of kisses later I said goodbye and drove home.

I checked to see if there was any footage and the screen was blank. That ruddy thing.

Back at the yard there had been quite a turnaround in liveries. Naomi had gone, very quickly in one afternoon after an argument with the owner over the quality of the hay.

So Pudding found himself with two new field mates. One was a cob, owned by a pleasant but arthritic impaired lady who was a fastidious poo picker. The other was a bay gelding, a sensitive soul who loved attention and would throw himself into a panic if left on his own. Pudding and the cob quickly started a romance and can often be found together gently nibbling the same blade of grass or standing discreetly in a corner grooming each other.

Into this mix then arrived a young three-year-old cob owned by a long procession of people we nicknamed The Syndicate. Every day three or four cars would pull into the yard and decant men, women, dogs and children in buggies who would all assemble together around the stable while this little horse was fed and groomed. Like the Borg, they all moved as one and left as one.

Up to this point, there had been a little routine set up where the arthritic lady and I would take turns to clean the field of poo. There were a couple of reasons for doing this: it was not a particularly big area and there would be no grass for them to eat if we did not shift it, poo attracts flies and worms, it also sours the grass. Up to this point, these rather older and wiser gentlemen had very specific places where they would defecate, spots that were close to the periphery of the field. This left the majority of the field uncontaminated and free for grazing. This young colt arrives and poos literally everywhere. And there's mountains of it.

It made sense to have a chat and see if the principle owner could help out. I was assured that there was a string of reasons why that would not be possible; she had a baby and could not manage poo picking, on top of which, her horse was brought in during the day so clearly the poo in the field was not his. This was news to me, horses don't poo at night? Now, I am a fairly tolerant woman, but I found it was really beginning to grate when six of them would be stood around chatting and then leave without lifting a single finger. Arthritis was incensed, it caused her a huge amount of pain to lift and push, so she had little sympathy with a clan of healthy young people who were fully capable, but totally unwilling. Sensing that we were unhappy with the situation, the owner decided to move the young colt into a neighbouring field with one other cob. She reported back that The Syndicate was happy with the new arrangement and that they might now consider poo picking.

Almost as quickly as they arrived, they decided to leave, and came one morning to collect the cob, all his belongings and moved to another yard. They left the field covered in poo and the owner of their last field mate the unenviable task of having to clean it all up.

It is actually one of those moments, when I was in the field with my wheelbarrow, that will remain with me forever. The summer months had brought with them a regular routine of pub hacks; every Thursday night anyone who wanted to go would be there, tacked up, mounted and the whole group would set off down the country lanes to the local pub. The younger and more agile members of the ride would dismount, collect the orders and money from each rider and return a short while later with a tray full of drinks. On one occasion I had a couple of G&Ts and felt ever so merry. I generally don't drink unless I am out with others, but on this particular evening I just felt in the mood. When it comes to drinking, I am not sure you could even call me lightweight; feather weight would be closer to it. I vaguely remember the hack back, slumped in the saddle while Pudding took on the role of responsible adult and got me home safely.

On this evening however, I did not want to go home. It was a balmy night and the sky had been a glorious burnished orange as we had turned back into the yard. I put Pudding in the field, returning moments later with the wheelbarrow to commence my shift poo picking. I must have been there for an hour or so, as the sun had set and in its place was one of the largest moons I had ever seen. I stood there in awe of it. The whole field was lit with moonlight and Pudding just glowed in its milky sheen. There was complete peace, only punctuated by the distant call of an owl.

There are times in life when you want to drink in the moment and that was one of them. Here I was, in the moonlight on a glorious summer evening, just absorbing the beauty and feeling so much love for the little horse that shone in the corner of the field. I was completely and utterly happy.

It did take a little explaining when I got home, as Phil could not figure out how I had gone for a pub hack at six and was rolling in at eleven.

Pub hacks aside, there was not that much riding happening during the week as most people were working. I was itching to do something, so I decided that I would negotiate Somerford farm ride on my own. I had already reached and passed so many milestones, so something within me needed to know I could do it. I could actually get Pudding round Somerford without anyone else and hopefully without incident.

One for the road, sharing my G&T with Pudding

There were enough miles under the belt to know how to ride Pudding, but I was pretty unsure how he would respond on his own.

I set the date and got going nice and early. Once I had paid, mounted and was on my way, it became clear that Pudding was operating at a much higher level of awareness that he usually does. Everything got a second glance and he often let out a quite audible whinny when we were near other horses. For the first time in a long time I felt really nervous and tied desperately to breathe deeply and keep the reins loose. We had a little trot while I tried to calm myself down and then we got to the water. After a bit of persuasion Pudding finally waded through and we trotted up the bank and around the corner to the log. I had decided the night before that I was going to jump it, so gaining some comfort from the fact I was wearing my enormous body protector, I nudged Pudding into canter and over we went. We cantered on for a little while and then slowed down to a trot as we approached the stairs. The last time I had descended these was on my first trip here, when the park was full, and Pudding was too excited by far, spinning this way and that when we had got to the bottom. Today the ride was deserted; something I had phoned ahead and checked on before I booked.

We approached the steps and Pudding stopped dead, refusing to go down. It was a lovely sunny day, which was great when you were out on the main track, but the steps led down into a bowl and the whole area was flanked with trees, which meant we were looking down into a black hole. I pushed and pushed him, but he just side stepped and refused to make any attempt to go forward. By now the nerves had gone and I was consumed with determination that he WAS going down the steps. Having read so many times that you cannot let a horse win an inch or he will constantly challenge you, in that moment I felt like it was the most important thing in the world to get that horse down those stairs. Pudding however, did not feel that the situation carried the same importance – all he could see was a black hole and for all he knew we were about to drop into a bottomless pit. In frustration I got off, grabbed the reins, stood on the first step and tried to pull him forward. What ensued was ten minutes of pulling, swearing, pulling and swearing. A brief pause to collect my breath, then a further five minutes of pulling and swearing. He moved not one inch forward.

With a red face and puffing like a steam train, I climbed up the step, walked him round to a log and mounted. He was perfectly happy to walk past the steps and we covered the next half mile with me sat aloft giving him 'the talk'. He settled into a steady walk, ears flicking this way and that, while I chunnered on about him needing to understand who is boss and when I ask him to do something, he needed to do it. I'm pretty convinced he was quietly thinking 'yeah right'.

Our event at the steps had blown the nerves away and we continued on with a happy mix of a couple of trots and the odd canter, both of us quite relaxed and settled. We were a few miles into the ride and making our way down a steep hill when Pudding started to move from side to side and get agitated. I could hear voices behind me, so I turned him round and we watched two glorious event horses shimmy down the track towards us, ridden by two immaculately turned out gentlemen. One was wearing a tweed jacket and the other taller fellow a silk jumper, both sat on their horses as though they had been born on them.

"I'm here on my own, first time" I chirped as they levelled with me "a bit nervous actually"

"Well you can tag along behind us if you like" quipped the silk jumper, without even looking round.

"I can trot, and canter but I would only want to gallop if we are going uphill" I shouted after him.

No response. So, I set off some distance behind them and marvelled at how beautifully the horses moved and how elegant they all looked. As they had gained quite a bit of ground I decided to let Pudding have a little canter to catch up. I shortened the reins and off we went, and went. I could see both riders getting closer and closer, so I signalled for Pudding to slow down and he finally skidded to a stop only a couple of feet behind them. Both horses jumped in the air and silk jumpers did a little buck. I got The Look.

"I'm so sorry, really I am"

No response. They picked up pace and began to trot off. This time I used every ounce of strength and kept Pudding firmly at a walk until they had disappeared out of view. For the second time that day he got 'the talk'.

Our final stretch was much better, we had a good gallop up the hills and some lovely canters along the track until, both covered in sweat, we had reached the end of the ride. Apart from our little event with the eventers, it had gone quite well I thought.

I was thankful that the headcam had worked and laughed when I got back, quite apart from the panting breath when we first started, I had no idea that I had such colourful language in my armoury.

It was some months later when I decided to tackle Somerford again on my own. The weather had been really bad, so most of the off-road hacking routes were flooded and pretty impassable. It was mid-week and I was desperate for a ride, so off we went.

This time both of us felt so much more relaxed, we had done this before and knew what to expect. The water was easy, then over the log. I didn't even bother with the steps, instead pushed on in trot just enjoying the fact that we had the park to ourselves and we were finally out and about. As we descended the same hill

Overheated and exhausted – and that's just me

Pudding became just as agitated as last time. I turned him round to see two horses cantering along the track above us, about to head in our direction.

"Can you slow down please" I shouted firmly

"Oh sorry" shouted the man "will do"

It looked like it was father and daughter out together and they said a brief hello as they passed. Once we were all at the bottom of the hill and they were a safe distance away, they picked up pace and cantered off. Pudding was becoming more and more restless as he could hear the sound of their hooves in the distance, I thought we might do a gentle little canter after them, but this turned out to be a huge mistake. He went into a full bolt, thundering down the track and around the corner to chase them up the hill. They had stopped and were quietly walking up when we shot around the corner, up the hill and ploughed through the centre of them sending both horses flying in either direction. I had no power to stop and found myself shouting in frustration

"I'm sorry, he's such a little f***er" as we thundered past.

Once at the top of the hill Pudding spotted the moving arm of a crane and stopped dead, sending me shooting forwards. I managed to scramble back into my saddle and apologised profusely to the couple as they walked past.

"Don't worry" said the man in a broad Yorkshire accent "you alright love?"
"I am, thanks" I replied.

I had no choice at this point but to continue with the ride, as we were a good few miles from the car park. There was no joy in this whatsoever. The bolt had disarmed me, and I really wanted the ride to end; but there was nothing I could do about the fact we were still so far from the van. We continued on the path, first down the gorge and then back up on the other side. I would usually let Pudding canter up this section, which he knew all too well. He was jogging about pulling me along, just waiting for me to give the all clear for take-off. I had no intention of flying Air Pudding again today, so we bounced along in walk all the way to the top.

There was a voice inside which kept telling me that I had to finish on a positive note; I had to try and detach from my emotions and focus on the simple mechanics of what I was doing. I detoured round and cut off the final section as Pudding was so revved up. As we jogged past the main arenas I spotted an empty one and directed him, we did circles for about twenty minutes until he calmed down and for the first time in over an hour we both relaxed.

Now felt like a good time to try and load him, so I walked over to the van, untacked and tried to get him in. He swung in every direction and bluntly refused to go up the ramp. I spotted the father and daughter parked a few vans away from me and went to ask if they could help me

"No love" he said without glancing in my direction "we are in a hurry, already late"

Fair enough, I had crashed through them, so I was not surprised they had no desire to delay their departure trying to help me get the source of the trouble into a horsebox.

I wandered off around the stables to see if there was anyone else. Two well-dressed ladies appeared and again I asked if they wouldn't mind giving me a quick hand

"I don't think so" said one and they both walked off.

Crickey, this was turning into quite a trial. Thankfully a gentleman who had been tending to his horse overheard our conversation and came to my rescue. He held the lunge rope out, so Pudding could not swing round when he got to the gate and the little fella was loaded in seconds.

Thank goodness for real gentlemen.

Now he was in the van I followed our routine and gave him a little feed. I stood there watching him munch, with clouds of steam rising through his cooler into the air around him. He had been literally dripping by the time we had finished the ride and clearly overheated with all the excitement. What a nugget.

That evening I contacted the teenager who had previously owned him to ask if she had ever experienced anything like his reaction today.

"Oh yes" she replied "he gets really scared when he can hear horse's hooves, especially if they are behind him. When we were out hunting I would dread anyone galloping up behind me, he would just want to bolt"

Horrified I replied "And what did you do?"

"Either try and get him in an outline to take his mind off it or if he goes for it, then sit back, press your feet into the stirrups and pull hard on the reins until he stops".

I guess it would just have to be 'sit back' for me, as I hadn't yet managed an outline when we were in the ménage, so it was highly unlikely he was suddenly going to throw a shape when something was galloping up behind him.

Chapter Ten

I opened my phone and read the text from Ruth, the local school were wondering whether we could take the horses in for the children to see. They had been running a piece on knights, so they felt it would be of real educational value to let the kids have a supervised session learning how to look after a horse, in the same way a knight would. I was very thankful that they had abandoned their original idea that we should demonstrate a jousting competition.

Pat a pony day

On the morning of the visit I was somewhat flustered. Having been away for a few days I had not got things set up quite the way I wanted, I like to make sure his tail is washed, and he has had a good groom. Just like any mum sending their baby to school, you want them to look their best. But time was tight, and we had to get cracking, or we would miss the first group. Ruth was riding Ebony and I was on Pudding, as they seemed to be the most sensible horses and we needed to ensure that no child would be kicked or bitten.

"We are going to have to trot" said Ruth staring at her watch "we've only got ten minutes to get there"

We picked up pace and trotted through the residential streets until we finally made it to the school, just minutes before the first class were due out. We were greeting by one of the organisers who told us to tie the horses to the fence on the small front lawn area next to the maple saplings and they would bring the children out.

Both horses stood there with ears flicking this way and that as the screams and chatter of thirty children suddenly broke the silence. With excitement they turned the corner and stood cooing at the horses in front of them. While one of the teachers began to explain the importance of looking after your horse, Ruth and I looked at each other

"I hope they are going to be OK" I whispered
"They'll be fine" she winked

Once divided into two groups they moved forward *en masse*, with some diving straight in to stoke and others cowering at the back looking absolutely terrified. Now this was something I could definitely handle, so I decided to get some structure to the session. I began by asking them to feel Pudding's furry coat and then his tail, so they could see the difference. I asked why his eyes were at the side of his head and not at the front like ours, then explained he had a blind spot right in front of his head, but he could see behind him, letting him watch out for lions that might want to eat him. We watched his ears flick all the way round so that he could hear sounds from any direction. I picked up his hooves, so they could see his feet and metal shoes.

The children were completely fascinated and even those who were frightened at first began to relax and join in. Pudding was completely chilled and not the slightest bit bothered by any of the attention, in fact, I think he quite enjoyed it. I waved goodbye to the group and turned to Ruth

"I really enjoyed that. They seemed so interested"
"Yep, it was good" she replied "just another fifteen groups to go"
"You're kidding" I gasped as the next bubble of screaming children appeared.

I have no idea how teachers manage to do it. The questions were never ending, the energy levels were sky high and trying to keep an eye on where everyone was, when children kept bobbing off, was exhausting. I was trying very hard not to be bothered by the fact children with candlesticks running from each nostril would routinely wipe themselves with the back of their hand them immediately stroke Pudding. I was discretely circling my pony with wet wipes whenever I got a moment.

During the midmorning break we took a chance to get a breather. We noticed that both horses had edged forward and on closer inspection they had worked their way through half the leaves and smaller branches on the maple saplings.

Telling a tale..

"Ruth, look at the trees. There's only half left"

"Crickey. They look like some sort of commemorative planting" she replied, examining them more closely

"Let's see if we can move the horses" I replied

We walked them over to the big tree in the centre of the lawn, but the trunk was too wide to secure them with the short lead ropes we had brought with us. After much deliberation and a few attempts at alternatives, we returned to our original spot. There was really nowhere else we could go.

By the time the next session kicked off, both horses had been to the toilet, twice. Trying to stop a group of excited children from running into a pile of poo added an extra element to an already packed agenda. The local paper arrived, and we spent two sessions getting photos and quotes from children and teachers ready to print in that evenings edition.

The morning flew and by lunchtime we must have entertained over two hundred children. It had been intense, but a huge amount of fun and there was an enormous amount of satisfaction in letting children, most of whom have never been near a horse before, have the opportunity to stroke one and learn a little bit more about them. It was a privilege to have been part of so many children's first memory.

"Ready for lunch?" I shouted over to Ruth
"I'm famished she replied"

We went to untie the horses and realised to our horror, that while we had been busy educating the children, the horses had been busy eating the saplings. All that was left was the small spindly trunk and the support stake– every side branch and leaf was gone.

It was hard to be cross with these two lovely ponies, they had just spent the last four hours being stroked and prodded by hundreds of children.

"If they say anything, we'll just buy them another" I said, turning Pudding for home.

A week later all the schools turned out for their summer break.

One great advantage of the school holidays was the fact Chrissy was around every day and after a few long discussions she decided that she would like to venture out with Pudding and I. The best route for a first-time hacker would be the lines; no roads, just a long stretch of track with the odd dog walker or cyclist. With Pudding as chaperon, we felt sure her horse Nacho would follow behind without any problems. To add to the occasion, we were going to bob to the pub at the end and meet up with Chrissy's grandparents.

We set off bright and early on a beautiful sunny day and in no time at all we were making good time along the track. As we suspected Nacho was calm and happy to follow Pudding; none of the various people or objects along the way presented any problems at all. Once we had reached the end of the lines, we made the short detour around to the pub where the grandparents were stood waiting for us

"We thought you'd got lost" said the grandmother
"I'm sorry, it took us a little longer than we thought it would. Have you been waiting long?" I replied

"About twenty minutes" returned the grandfather "but that's not the bad news. I'm afraid the pub doesn't open until six on Fridays"

Chrissy and I looked at each other, we had spent the last twenty minutes in joyful anticipation of a long cool drink. All was not lost, someone must have been looking down on us with pity that day, as a young lady appeared out of nowhere and stood by the door fiddling with a set of keys. We explained the situation to her and after a pause she declared

Refreshed and ready for the journey home

"I'm going to get killed for this, but if you hold on a minute then I will get you a drink"

She was as good as her word, we all got refreshments and I sat back in my saddle enjoying a glorious G&T. So far everything had gone to plan, and we were feeling rather pleased with ourselves; which proved to be a touch premature. Chrissy had jumped off to sit on a bench and enjoy her drink, while Nacho in his quest to reach the grass had trod on his rein, which promptly snapped in two. And it was not an even break, one side had only a few inches of leather, so there was no possible way she could hack back using it. We were immediately thrown into action and I was blown away by the simple 'sort it' mentality of this spritely pair of pensioners. Directing operations, the grandfather pointed at the belt around his wife's waist and within seconds, with one hand holding her loose fit linen pants, she handed it over. I presume he had been a sailor (or possibly a boy scout leader) as he then tied a set of intricate knots securing the belt to the bridle. Standing back to review his work, he declared that Nacho was now 'fit to ride'. The wife, trousers in hand, concurred.

This was the Baby Boomer generation who just got on with things and I loved them for it. Any Generation Y faced with the same situation would have spent the first ten minutes having a dramatic meltdown and then the next twenty minutes texting all their friends and posting pictures on Facebook.

Chrissy was a little shaken at the thought she had four miles to ride with only a thin strip of M&S belt as a means of control, but there was no way around it, we just had to make the best of it. Once back in the saddle we turned for home and did a final farewell to the grandparents. For the briefest moment the grandma forgot and both hands went aloft for a big farewell wave, until she suddenly remembered and grabbed her trousers before there was any chance she could be arrested for indecent exposure.

We walked steadily back to the van, finding the funny side of our predicament and agreeing that we would do another ride next week. Which was exactly what we did, only this time I chose a route that involved little sections of road work, which Nacho handled without any problem at all. We were all becoming a little more relaxed having him out and about; with a sensible chaperon he behaved himself beautifully. Chrissy was beginning to relax which made the whole experience so much more enjoyable for both of us.

I found myself completely absorbed by the whole experience of riding Pudding. Many an evening I would sit with Phil who thought I was watching TV with him, but I was often in a world of my own, reliving a previous ride or imagining a future one. It was not unusual for me to spend hours on the iPad looking at up and coming events, trying to decide which would be good to have a go at. I tried to explain it to Phil, who wanted to get his head around it – the 'thing' that happens inside you when you ride. There is a connection that is nothing like anything else I have experienced. A dog, for example, is a separate unit and as much as you may love them, they operate independently to you. It's not like that with a horse; you move together, anticipate each other, you become one unit. There is trust between you, shared moments of enjoyment at new experiences or places and a united adrenaline rush when you have picked up speed and had a good gallop. I have heard it said that happiness comes from doing things for others; which is probably why there are so many happy horse owners. It all centres around 'doing' for your horse; ensuring they are warm , fed, in good health and emotionally stimulated. Caring for them is like looking after a small child, it is constant and in the back of your mind all the time, even when you are not with them. It is not a wonder that most horse owners will drop everything for the chance to do something with their horse.

It was the same for Janet and I. And as we were now becoming a lot more confident about taking the van out and exploring new places, it became a frequent event and one we both looked forward to. After watching a YouTube clip of a ride around Delamere forest, I suggested that we give it a go and Janet was in full agreement.

It had been raining all week and everything felt damp and muddy underfoot. As we set off in the van we decided that we would probably take it easy, as we didn't want the horses to slip and injure themselves. It took nearly an hour to get there, so we were quite relieved to pull into the large car park and get going. We were now entering October and the whole forest was bursting with Autumnal colour; reds, oranges and burnished copper colours met the eyes wherever you looked. We followed the path through the woods, chatting happily, only pausing to say hello to the walkers we passed along the way.

"There is a place called Old Pale" I said "where apparently you can see four counties. Do you fancy giving it a go?"
"Yes please" returned Janet "that sounds lovely"

It is one thing knowing that something is there, but quite another finding it. The forest was huge, with no signs to tell you where anything was, or whether you were travelling in the right direction towards it; if you are not careful you can easily end up just doing endless circuits around the lake. I announced that I was going to ask someone, so we could get a handle on where it was. As the next walker approached, I stopped Pudding and made the enquiry

"Excuse me, do you have any idea which direction we need to take to get to Old Pale?
"No" came the reply.

Fair enough, I would just ask again until we found someone who knew. With each blank it was not long before my enquiry had been stripped to the bare bones.

"Excuse me, do you have any idea which direction we need to take to get to Old Pale?"
"Excuse me, do you know the way to Old Pale?"
"Do you know the way to Old Pale?"
"Old Pale?"

I felt I had morphed into a Victoria Wood character, the one who stops everyone she meets asking 'have you seen my sister?'
I was doing that to all passers-by "Old Pale?" "Old Pale?"
We eventually circled round to the car park, with me still barking "Old Pale?" to anyone and everyone. To our delight a rather foxy gentleman knew exactly where it was and gave us

directions. I had turned and was walking away before I realised that I was on my own, Janet was still engrossed in giggly chatter behind me. I caught her eye and she nodded, then continued as before. A few giggles later she said farewell and finally caught up with me

"He was lovely" she grinned

"I can't take you anywhere" I replied.

Once we had reached the top of Old Pale we stopped, amazed at the view. You could see as far as the Welsh mountains, we then turned our heads to catch the oil refineries with their tall chimneys billowing steam, then the flat Cheshire plains and Jodrell Bank in the far distance. We tried to ignore the enormous telephone masts someone had stuck up there and enjoy the panorama around us.

"It's amazing just how much you can see" said Janet, as together we tried working out the geography in front us. There was a moment when Pudding caught my eye, he seemed just as fascinated by the view as we were.

In the distance we could see a big black rain cloud, so we decided to turn back. Once inside the forest there were tracks and paths criss-crossing each other in every direction. We pootled on, picking the ones which looked like the best option for the horses and hopefully in the right direction to the car park. It was not long before we realised that we were completely lost. I began a fresh line of enquiry with every passer by

"Excuse me, do you have any idea which direction we need to take to get to Whitefield Car Park?"

"Excuse me, do you know the way to Whitefield Car Park?"

"Do you know the way to Whitefield Car Park?"

"Whitefield Car Park?"

After a lengthy detour on the road flanking the forest, we eventually found our missing car park and were happily reunited with the van. A short while later two very happy ladies were walking out of their favourite petrol station with coffee and pastries. After all, it had been quite an exhausting morning.

It was almost a week later, and I found myself itching to get out on a ride. Normally I take Pudding to the lines when I ride alone, as I know it's nice and safe, but I was bored with the route and longed for something more exciting. I decided that I would return to Delamere and even though I would be on my own, I felt sure I would be OK. I packed Pudding into the van and set off, with the entire journey taken up with the 'conversation' in my head. One voice was telling me this was utter madness and I should not be attempting anything so adventurous on my own; the other voice simply said, 'shut up and do it'. I pulled into the car park and to my absolute delight there was another horsebox there, with two riders who were starting to unload their horses. Bingo! I quickly parked next to them and strode over to introduce myself – I had every intention of riding with them, whether that was part of their plans or not. It transpired that it was their first time at Delamere and they were unsure of the route

"No problem" I assured them "I can take you to Old Pale, it's a fantastic view across the forest and beyond"
To my great relief they liked the idea and we tacked up and set off.

Now the thing about promising someone that you will show them the way, is that you do actually need to know the way. It became pretty evident quite quickly that I did not really have any great grasp on where we should be going. In my defence, I thought I remembered the route, but suddenly all the paths looked the same and the last time I rode this we only found our way after getting hideously lost. I bluffed my way through until to my great relief we stumbled across the visitor's centre, having done a long and winding detour to get there. From that point it was a straight trek to the top.

I found much enjoyment in riding and chatting with these ladies. Kathy was closer to my age and had been riding for years, she had an impeccably behaved Connemara which she rode with elegance. We discovered that she only lived a short distance away from me and was free during the week, so she could come out hacking with me. I had no idea at this point the pivotal part she would play in future events. Her companion was a vet who was enjoying a rare day off from work and spent most of the time figuring out the route after we had reached the top of Old Pale and I abandoned the role of trek leader. I was very happy to follow her direction and as we passed the visitor centre I was genuinely surprised just how close it was to the car park actually was. Who knew?

Once we were back at the vans it was time to get loaded. There were now other horses dotted around the car park which obviously caught Pudding's eye and he was zoned in to every noise and movement. I should have picked up on this and thought the next steps through, as I know Pudding gets fizzy when he can hear other horses moving about in the distance. But I had decided that the best thing I could do was to get him in the van as quickly as possible which proved to be a huge mistake. I untied the lead rope, gathering it in my hand and began to circle him round to face the van, just as the we heard the very audible clatter of horse's hooves on the loading ramp of another van and without a second glance Pudding pulled away and was off. Really off – out of the car park and down the road. I ran after him as and I reached the car park entrance I could see him in the distance still going at quite a pace. I was terrified he was going to get hit by a car, so I ran into the middle of the road and flung my arm out to stop the traffic. The first car stopped obligingly, but the motorbike behind him decided that he would overtake and swung round directly in front of me. Steely resolve hit me, and I flung myself in front of him with my arm stretched out and the flat palm of my hand in the STOP position. His eyes caught mine and he stopped dead. I was not to be messed with today.

To my relief a small transit van had pulled up much further down on the other side of the road and the driver had kindly got out to stop the traffic in the other lane. Gathering all my energy I ran and as the distance passed, I jogged and then eventually walked panting until I finally caught up with my now stationary horse. It transpired that he had travelled quite some distance before deciding to slow down to a walk. An elderly gentleman had been stood next to the side of the road leaning on his walking stick whilst waiting for his lift, as Pudding ambled passed he had reached out and taken the line in his hand and now both man and horse were just stood on the spot waiting for back up.

I thanked him profusely, grabbed Pudding and began the long walk back the car park. Within minutes the vet appeared and looking at my red and sweat covered face, asked if I would like her to take over

"yes please" I replied gratefully

She grabbed the rope and frog marched him down the path, every time he went to look at something he got a jerk on the rope and a stern word. His head lowered, he knew she meant business, which she most definitely did. He was marched into the car park and straight into the van. I was now physically and emotionally exhausted, while I slumped next to the van to regroup, Pudding calmly commenced with his hay net as though nothing had happened.

To my astonishment Kathy was still happy to hack out with me and we exchanged numbers. I cannot imagine many people, seeing a potential hacking partner chase their horse down a main road, would have thought they were a good option to ride out with – but I am very grateful that she did.

A few weeks later we met for a local amble around the country lanes. Her horse had quite a pace and I had to routinely trot to catch up. As we chatted I invited her to tell me when she could see things that I needed to improve on. Now the great thing about Kathy is that she is a straight talker, so the invitation was accepted, and I was quickly enrolled into the Kathy School of Better Horsemanship. It was a bit of a shock at the amount of stuff I needed to work on; getting Pudding to walk at a faster pace, getting him to listen and act the first time I asked him to do something, my rogue left leg, not slumping in my saddle but actually sitting up and riding

"You are currently a passenger and you need to be a rider" she remarked.

It would be so easy to remain in the comfortable place I had been in; Pudding and I could hack just about anywhere, we were a little close unit. But without doubt, I had let a lot slip and plateaued in my riding education. I knew this was going to be hard, but I would embrace everything Kathy told me and work hard to get better.

Chapter Eleven

It crossed my mind that Delamere would be a good place to take Chrissy for our next outing, so I broached it with her mother when we found ourselves stood in the hay barn together one evening.

"Do you think Nacho will be alright there?" she pondered "Chrissy's not done anything that adventurous before"
"I do" I replied "I think he will be absolutely fine"
"OK then, but let's not tell her where she's going until we need to, or she will panic"

It was a week later in the van to Delamere that Chrissy turned to me and asked me directly

"Where are we going Caroline?"
"Delamere" I replied cautiously, realising that no one had told her yet.

She stared at me, then pushed back in her seat looking horrified.

"I'm not sure, will there be open spaces?"
"Nope" I replied "It's one big path all the way around. You'll be fine. Stop panicking"

There was a moment pause, with raised eyebrows, she quickly turned her head in my direction

"Did my mum know?"

"I think I might have mentioned it to her" I replied cautiously

Within a split second the phone was out of her pocket and she was dialling. In a perfectly calm voice she waited until her mum had said hello

"I can't believe you didn't tell me"

"You'd have only worried" her mum replied

"Mmmm"

After a brief chat about the contents of her packed lunch, which to our delight contained two chocolate mini-rolls, the phone went down and for the first time she smiled. Resigned to her fate.

It was the most glorious morning, warm, sunny and bursting with autumnal colour. Once we were on our way Chrissy soon relaxed as Nacho assumed his usual position behind Pudding and we walked gently along with Chrissy chatting merrily. We laughed at odd shaped trees, loved the way the lake glistened in the sunshine and enjoyed the 'oo's' and 'ahh's' from the young children when they saw the horses. We knew that there was a GoApe in Delamere, so we were on the lookout for zip wires and Segway's; and it wasn't long before we saw a group of Segway's in front of us, so we stopped the horses to let them take a proper look. It was half term break and there were quite a few families in the woods today enjoying different pursuits; walking, bike riding, picnics and the GoApe activities. The two families before us were clearly on Segway's for the first time, the mothers cautiously edged along while the men and boys were already trying the patience of the instructor as they raced each other down the path. Seeing the horses, the instructor directed them into a clearing and without a second glance the horses walked past. Chrissy was delighted, Nacho was doing really well, and she was beginning to actually enjoy the ride.

We were even more impressed with Nacho when we realised that we had stopped under one of the aerial walkways and there were people clambering along directly above us. He did nothing, although we decided to get both horses moving on just in case he changed his mind.

We continued on until we noticed the tree we were sure we had joked about earlier in the ride, was it possible that we had just done one giant loop around the lake? After taking directions we took at narrow track which led to the main car park and café area. Pudding knew where he was, he had been here a couple of weeks before and pottered on happily, ignoring the children playing, cyclists whizzing past and other various commotion.

The horses seem to be enjoying all the activity, I guess it can be just as interesting for them to get out and see different things.

Our final stretch was obviously to the top of Old Pale and got there in no time at all. Today was sunny and bright and the view stretched for miles

"Wow' said Chrissy

"I know" I replied "It's amazing"

We had a joke with a cyclist who we had passed in the car park, as he had

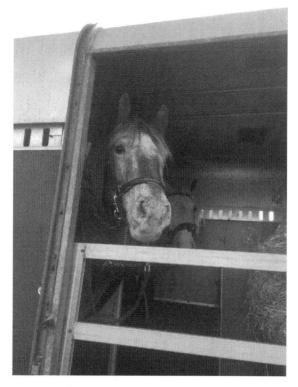

A room with a view

somehow managed to make it to the top ahead of us; then we turned and worked our way back down.

Once we were in the van going home, Chrissy was glowing with a sense of achievement. She deserved to be happy, she had faced her fear and taken a young, inexperienced horse out to somewhere with a million different things for him to freak at; but she had ridden it and ridden it well.

"Let's do it again on my next break from school"

"Sure thing" I replied

The next break was the Christmas one. For weeks before the weather had been terrible, heavy rains, a four-day snow blizzard and generally very unpleasant conditions. The horses had been forced to spend a lot of time stuck in their stables, as there were times when the fields were flooded, or the ground underfoot was just too icy for them to safely walk on. They were generally bored, and you could sense there was a build-up of energy, so they were likely to go off like a bottle of pop the moment you put them in the field.

Nacho was definitely one to watch after long spells in the stable. He was a chunky moorland pony who was built to survive in the wild quite happily living on bits of scrubland with meagre amounts of food. So long periods in the stable where he had constant access to hay cranked his excitability to off the chart levels. He would get giddy and want to just 'go', popping in the odd buck for good measure.

There had been a week where the bad weather seemed to break, and we had a mild spell, so everyone was keen to get out and do something. Chrissy was no different, she had been for a hack around the block with another livery during the week and wanted to go out again at the weekend. I was more than happy to oblige, it was always fun to take a pootle with her. I arrived at the stable and she was already in the ménage with Nacho, while her mum leant against the fence and watched. I loved Chrissy's mum Beverley, she was level headed, kind, fun to talk to and one of the most genuine people I had ever met.

"We are not as relaxed this morning" said Bev, greeting me with a smile

"Why, what's up?" I enquired just a Chrissy pulled up next to us

"He's being an idiot this morning, I don't know what's wrong with him" she said firmly

"What is he doing?" I continued

"He's bucked and he's just pulling me around"

"Do you still want to take him out" I enquired, thinking that she would probably not want to bother

"Oh, yes" she replied "let's go around the block"

I looked at the restless Nacho and had a small sense of foreboding in my stomach "Are you sure you wouldn't prefer to go down the lines instead? No traffic"

"No, round the block will be fine" she replied.

I headed off to get Pudding tacked up and returned a short while later

"Ok then, let's go"

"I'll follow in the car" said Bev, probably sensing that we may need assistance.

We walked down the drive, out of the front gates and were literally ten metres down the road when a large lorry pulled up behind us with the engine revving and the hiss of hydraulic brakes literally feet away from us. Nacho began to dart this way and that across the road in fear, with Chrissy fighting to control him

"Caroline" shouted Chrissy desperately

To my astonishment the lorry was actually a horsebox – I couldn't believe that anyone who understood anything about horses would drive so recklessly. I felt a sense of panic, there was nowhere for us to go. The lorry was that wide there was only a narrow gap between it and the hedge, so it was not possible to get the horses past it and back to the yard and there were no pavements or any area we could pull into to let it pass. We would have to hack down the road to the first house about one hundred metres along and swing into that driveway. As we began to walk on, Nacho was getting more and more agitated and despite my gestures asking the driver to pull back, the horsebox just kept edging on right behind us.

"Let's trot it" shouted Chrissy
"Are you sure" I shouted back

Nacho looked almost ready to bolt, so Chrissy managed to get him behind Pudding and we trotted down the road in an attempt to get into the drive as quickly as possible. On reflection there are quite a few things we should have done but trotting down was not one of them.

It felt like an eternity before we finally reached the driveway and turned in. The horsebox passed with one final hiss from the brakes and within a split-second Chrissy was off and Nacho was bolting around the garden. In full gallop he did one circuit after another round the lawn, then he headed towards the driveway just as Bev pulled her car across it, seeing his exit was now blocked he screeched to a halt, turned back on himself and set off again round and round the lawn.

I had pulled Pudding back, but he was now putting in a series of little excited jumps, this looked like a great game and he clearly wanted to join in

"Get off" shouted Bev firmly. So I did.

We took a moment to watch Nacho as he circled past us and absorbed the full horror of what was happening. Turf was flying up in the air to the left and the right and believe me, this was no ordinary turf. We had pulled into the garden of one of the most well-kept and immaculate lawns in whole of Cheshire. It was one long stretch of velvet smooth green, you felt you would need lawn slippers just to walk on it.

Nacho began to calm down and had settled into short trots, a brief stop then another short trot.
"you hold Pudding" I said " and I'll go and get him"

I handed the reins over and was half way across the lawn when Pudding sped past me in full gallop. Delighted to have company Nacho jumped into action and the two of them began circuits around me.

"I'm sorry" came a voice from behind me "he pulled away".

I stood chilled to the very core of my being as I watched both horses gallop around me, taking in every square foot of lawn; a couple of times around the rose beds, then back over to the arbour; a fly past the back fence and vegetable patch, round the perimeter of the lawn again and a several darts across it. As one slowed down, the other would speed past and the whole thing would begin again. All three of us just stood there like stone statues, helpless to do anything to stop the mayhem that was happening in front of us.

After what felt like an eternity they eventually slowed down at the very end of the garden on the top of a bank which butted onto the back fence. Pudding had somehow managed to get his rein caught on one of the fence posts and I was terrified that he would try and gallop off and rip his mouth. I edged towards him trying to reassure him until I was close enough to grab the rein and unhook him. Without any sort of fight he walked down the bank next to me and across the lawn. Chrissy had followed me across the lawn and was able to grab Nacho who was thoroughly exhausted and covered in sweat. We just stood there, holding the horses, mortified at the carnage before us. There was not a single square foot that hadn't been churned over or trampled on. Gone was the pristine lawn and in its place was something that resembled the track after the Grand National. We looked at each other, absolutely speechless. There were no words needed; there was a horrifying reality dawning on us. The unstoppable inevitability of that moment when the owner returns home and the mushroom cloud goes up. We were going to get blasted into the stratosphere.

There was no way we were going to ride those horses back, so I left Pudding with Beverley while I ran back, collected the van and Fleur. After some feisty resistance from Pudding we did eventually manage to get both horses into the horsebox and drove them the short distance back to the yard. Once safely in their stables we regrouped to discuss what exactly we were going to do next.

"I think we should go back and put a note through the letterbox straight away" said Bev "so they know we intend to sort things out and not just leave it that way"
"That's the best option" I replied "I've got a notepad in the van, so I will write a letter out now and put it through the door when I drive past"

I was relieved that there were still no cars in the driveway as I crept up to the door, put the note through the letterbox and ran full speed back to the car.

It was about an hour later when my phone went, and I answered to a rather prim ladies voice
"I believe your horses have been running amuck in my garden" she began
"I'm so very *very* sorry" I replied " we are absolutely mortified"
"Well I was at church this morning. It was my son who phoned to say he had received a few calls from friends who had passed the house and seen horses running around the garden"
She continued "I presumed they must have come from your livery yard, so I phoned them, and they gave me your number"
"Oh" I said "so you've not seen the note I pushed through the door"

"No, I have not seen a note" she replied "We never use the front door anyway"

I had a strange sense that she had literally just walked in and picked up the phone

"Have you been out in the garden yet?" I asked tentatively

"Not yet. I will go and have a look in a minute" she replied

We then had a brief discussion about the events of the morning and I assured her that we would make good her lawn, agreeing with her that it would obviously need to be to the same standard as before. I hung up and said a quick prayer that at church that morning the vicar had spoken at length on the very real benefits of forgiveness. And that she would reflect on this before she stepped out of her back door and gazed over the remains of her garden.

Chapter Twelve

As the winter progressed there were fewer and fewer organised rides. I scoured the various websites and Facebook pages and found a bridleways association in the next county who had a couple of rides still running – so I promptly booked myself on. I had every intention of going on my own, as neither Janet or Ruth could make the date. But as the ride got closer I began to get nervous and decided to put a message out on the yard Facebook page. I was delighted when the livery yard owner said her daughter would like to come with me. I had ridden with Grace before and he was a very capable rider with a calm, kind natured cob.

The morning of the ride arrived, and I knew we had to be setting off by 8am in order to get there for the advised 9am start time. I had stuck my head around the stable door to check that Grace was getting ready and she assured me that everything was in hand. By quarter to eight I had put everything was in the van and Pudding was ready to load, so I checked on Grace again

"How's it going?" I enquired
"Nearly there" she replied "I am just plaiting her mane"
"OK. Well I'm ready, so just let me know when you are finished, and we can get going".

This was pretty much the same conversation at 8.10, 8.15 and 8.20, until she finally emerged from the stable with a beautifully turned out horse, looking very pleased with her efforts and completely unaware of the knots of stress which had formed on my face.

Once we had eventually loaded the horses and Grace had bobbed back for numerous random items she suddenly remembered she needed, we were finally on our way.

It was just over an hour later, and nearly forty-five minutes after the start time, we pulled into Sugnall Walled Garden. A bright and friendly official was there waiting for us

"You are the last ones now" she said "But don't worry. The field is quite muddy, so I suggest that you park over there" pointing to a grass verge.

I moved the van into position and ran around to unload Pudding, just as the bullocks in the field all raced over and stuck their heads over the hedge to see what was happening. My heart skipped a beat, Pudding was half way down the exit ramp being led towards them, with upwards of twenty bullocks only feet away from him. He stopped, looked at them and then thankfully decided that he wasn't bothered today and continued without any drama. To our utter relief Grace's horse did exactly the same.

Finally in the saddle, we were off and carefully examining the route map for directions.

"This doesn't look too bad" I remarked "We only have six bullet points, so we should be around in no time"

"I have my compass with me if we need it" replied Grace

"Really, I didn't know you had a compass"

"It's a special app on my phone. I'm doing geography at school, so this will be the first time I have used it in a real situation" she smiled

"Wow. Well there's no way we are going to get lost then" I nodded.

To our delight we noticed pink ribbons tied to hedges or gates at key points when we had a turn to make.

We had travelled about a mile when we came to our first fork on the track and the instructions said, 'turn left'.

"It's this way" I said pointing to the path ahead

"I don't think it is" replied Grace

"It says 'turn left' and this is left" I said pointing to the instructions

"I know, but the bridlepath sign points that way" she said, indicating a right turn.

"Well, maybe we are not going down the bridlepath" I returned

We looked for pink ribbons and there were none, so after bickering for a few more minutes she conceded, and we turned left. Marching on I began to notice that the track was quickly becoming simply two strips of tyre tracks, until we rounded a corner and saw a farm yard directly ahead of us.

"I don't think this is it" I said

"mmm" said Grace with 'I told you so' written all over her face.

We turned back until we eventually joined the original fork and continued along the track taking the right turn.

"I have a compass reading, so we know where we are" remarked Grace

"Glad you do. At least one of does" I replied

About ten minutes on we were stopped dead in our tracks by an enormous tree trunk which had fallen, its branches spread from one side of the path to the other.

"This can't be right" said Grace "how are we supposed to get past this?"

We edged closer to have a look and found that the trunk was still connected to the tree by what appeared to be the thinnest splinter of wood. If it broke, it would send the bulk of the currently suspended branch crashing to the ground.

"I don't like this" I said

"There must be a way through, how did everyone else do it?" replied Grace.

We looked around for gates and there were none. We read the instructions again, it seemed like we had another mile or so on the bridlepath; so, in desperation I phoned the steward

"There seems to be a great big tree trunk across the bridlepath" I began "Is that right?"

"Yes, you are on the right route. Just go around it" came the reply

"Round it" I gasped

"Yes, everyone else has gone around it. There is another steward waiting at the entrance to the private land, as you are the last ones she can lock the gate once you are through"

I sensed that there were a few people who needed to be elsewhere, who were currently hanging around waiting for us.

"OK, we are on our way" I said hanging up.

"Round it" I confirmed to Grace.

We pushed our horses as close to the fence as possible and urged them on. They picked their way forward, as we ducked and dived to avoid branches; refusing point blank to look up. If this thing was going to fall I certainly did not want to see it.

Picking up the pace we continued along the track and then out onto the road for another few miles until we eventually saw a lady stood waiting by her car. As soon as we got close enough she began to jog down the track which spurred to the left of the road. I was in awe of her fitness, she jogged down the whole mile long track opened the gate at the end.

"Enjoy your ride" she said waving, before turning to jog back.

"Where are we now" I asked Grace

She examined the instructions and confirmed that we were now on a privately-owned piece of land that provided a long stretch for a 'lovely canter'. This was the bit I had been looking forward to, so after confirming that Grace was OK we nudged the horses into action. Pudding began in a steady canter and then gathered pace until we were enjoying a glorious gallop to the end. Grace and her mare joined us a few moments later, they had been much slower across the field and arrived plait still in place looking completely unruffled.

We went through the gate, down a passageway and onto the road, both of us pulling out our instructions to check where we should be going next. To our horror we realised that we were still on point one.

"dear god" I exclaimed "And how long have we been riding for now?"
"Nearly two hours" whispered an equally horrified Grace
"And we are still one point one?" I gasped

We looked at each other aghast.

"At this rate we still have another ten hours riding ahead of us" I mouthed, audible speech now having completely left me.

We sat there just looking at each other for a few moments. Trying to figure out our options, we had no choice but to continue. There was no way we could retrace our steps, gate behind us was now locked and there was also *the branch* to consider, neither of us fancied going past that again.

Grace got her compass out and we got serious. This was us against the elements, ride warriors, we were going to take on this thing and win.

We marched down the road with a determined stride, arms in the air and whoops of joy whenever we saw the next pink ribbon.

Pushing on we progressed through gates, across streams, down tracks and across fields until we made it to point 3, Bishops Wood. Our instructions advised us that this was an opportunity for another canter, but we decided that we would see how it went. For my part, whilst the mind was willing, the body was already at crunch point. Actually, not so much the body but the ankles. My legs ached, feet felt numb and my ankles felt weak, as though they might give way if I put too much pressure on them. I felt that it was only fair on Pudding that I should sit out of the saddle for any canter work, which meant that my legs and ankles would need to support me. I looked again at the instructions, we still had quite a distance to go, it made sense to try and cover as much ground as possible, for all our sakes. So as we turned into Bishops Wood we decided to have a canter. Unsurprisingly Pudding was not as full of beans as last time, but he picked up pace and we covered some ground before the pain in my ankle became too great and we had to slow down to a walk.

This was one of the truly frustrating things about getting older. I have no idea at what point I stopped being able to do anything and everything I wanted. The lines are blurred, you can't pinpoint it, gradually you are aware that something you could do without a second thought, you are now finding requires a lot of thought. Opening jam jars for example. When was it that I suddenly needed a gadget for the really tight ones? I never needed a gadget in my twenties or thirties. I really don't' like the fact I am now a Saga qualifying gadget lady.

The long-awaited gallop

One thing that age has taught me, is that success or failure is a mind game. The battle field is in your head, if you give up there, you have well and truly lost. And battle I did that afternoon, there was a part of me just wanted to phone someone to say, 'come get me, I'm done'. But accompanying me was a lovely young lady who was still enjoying her ride and putting her trust in me to look after her, so gathering any last scraps of stamina I could find we pressed on.

The final miles of the ride are a bit of a blur. Thankfully points five and six were nowhere near as long as their predecessors and just after three o'clock we finally turned the last corner and commenced with a steady plod towards the van. It was like a scene from a western movie, when the heroes who had been lost in the wilderness for days, finally make their way back to the ranch for a joyful reunion with their kinsfolk. Our steward had waited faithfully for our return and looked overjoyed and immensely relieved that all her charges were now safely accounted for.

After a few pleasantries we packed up and made our way back to the yard. After depositing the horses back in their stables, I drove home, had a warm bath and was in bed for eight thirty.

Winter had well and truly set in; the rain was relentless and there were frequent bouts of strong winds. One particular Saturday was very bad and the prospect of bringing Pudding across from the field was a daunting one. Ruth had bought a new horse, a four-year-old gelding; such a laid back happy little chap who was now sharing the field with Pudding. This had been quite a development for Pudding, as he was always skirting the bottom of the pecking order whenever he had shared with other horses, but he had asserted himself as the pack leader and seemed almost fatherly in determination to keep this younger cob in check.

After an exchange of texts Ruth and I decided to meet at the yard and bring both horses at the same time. We expected that they would be jumpy and easily spooked by the winds, so it would be much better to tackle it together. I absolutely hated the walk over when it was this kind of weather, no matter how many times I did it, it filled me with dread. This was magnified by the information Ruth and her daughter were now sharing with me as we strode across the road to the field

"He's really been quite a handful over the last few days" she said "I think it is the food balancer I have been feeding him"

"Has he had balancer before?" I enquired

"No, the vet told me to give him a handful, but I think its sending him a bit nuts"

We opened the gate and walked the short way down the track to the gate. Pudding was a few feet away and trotted up. Ruth's horse Puzzle was at the bottom of the field. He stood for a moment looking at us and then began a mad gallop to the top, almost crashing into the fence, followed by a series of bucks, circles, rearing, jumping and galloping in larger circles. The three of us just stood there like horrified hikers who have stumbled across a bear in the woods. In unison we took a step back and remained rooted to the spot.

"I'm not going in there" said Ruth

"Me neither" I replied

We continued to stand motionless, watching the theatrics continue without any sign of him slowing down. Occasionally Puzzle would come close to Pudding, who would turn and try to corral him into the corner, but Puzzle would pick up speed and whizz off, leaving Pudding like the rest of us – just stood there watching with incredulity.

"I'll go and get help" I said, turning to run back to the yard.

Once through the gates I saw Fleur and threw myself at her

"You've got to come over Fleur, Puzzle's gone nuts"

After a quick briefing on the situation we raided the tack room for Puzzle's bridle and ran back to Ruth and her daughter. They had not moved from where I left them, but thankfully Puzzle seemed to be calming down. With quiet confidence Fleur walked into the field, flanked Puzzle and with a couple of rapid movements had the bridle firmly in place. Puzzle seemed to know the game was up, he lowered his head and began to walk back towards the gate with Fleur leading him. This was the first time I felt remotely safe going into the field, so I quickly put the head collar on Pudding and we opened the gate to escort them out.

A huge gust of wind blew, shaking the hedge next to us; Puzzle jumped back and spun round with Pudding following. Both horses now seemed very agitated, with wild eyes and heads raised high.

"just keep walking" instructed Fleur

So that is what we did, we literally marched through the gate, down the road and onto the yard; ignoring every little side spin and jump forward. My heart was still racing a good while after Pudding was in his stable and settled. It was cold, wet, windy and horrible and I felt thoroughly fed up. I had booked to go on an endurance ride the following day, but there was not a cat in hells chance that I was going to take Pudding on a ride when he was that spooky. Especially when I was going on my own. I had been really looking forward to it, as there had been little real riding for weeks and I was desperate to get out and about. Feeling totally dejected I drove home.

I woke at 4am, bright and wide awake. I went downstairs, made a cup of tea and sat looking out of the window. It was still pretty dark, but there were all the signs that this was going to be a crisp January morning with no wind. I checked my weather app, then google, then another weather app. There was no rain, no wind and no snow for today. After an hour I decided that I was going to go; so as quietly as I could, I showered, got dressed and drove to the yard. Pudding was stood up asleep in his stable, his bottom lip hanging limply down, and his eyes half closed. In fact, every horse looked the same, all still fast asleep. After collecting the keys, I drove the van around to the side of the barn and as quickly as I could, got the tack and Pudding's dinner packed inside. I now had a lovely little routine in place, Pudding would get his food after a ride when he was loaded in the van. The sight of his little purple feed bowl would often be the decider on whether he was going to load easily or be a pain; it would catch his eye and he would happily march in behind me.

By the time I went back into the barn every horse was awake, with their heads craning over the stable doors top see what was going on. I put a travel rug on Pudding and led him out with the eyes of every horse on the aisle watching jealously. It felt like the closing scene from 'An officer and a Gentleman' when Richard Gere walks in, collects Debra Winger and they leave together to the sound of cheers and the odd 'way to go'.

Once on the road I looked at the time, it was now eight o'clock and it had been advised that most riders should be away by nine. I hit the motorway and raced along doing a steady sixty, the highest speed I had ever driven with Pudding. We arrived just after nine and there were only a few riders left, which sent a slight shot of panic through my body. I had really wanted to ride with someone else, it was enough that I didn't know the area or the route without heaping the additional drama of riding a horse who will be a whole heap more uptight on his own. The steward seemed to understand when I explained and told me to come with her, while she tried to get it sorted.

"This is Beverley" she said, introducing me to an older rider standing next to her grey Arab "this lady is looking for someone to ride with, would you mind?"
Beverley took one look at me, then Pudding and replied firmly "I am going to be going at some speed today. I think you had better find someone else"

The steward looked a little taken aback, as was I, so we walked back to find someone else. There were only two riders left, so we approached and gave it another go

"Ladies, would you mind if this lady rode with you? Everyone else has gone and she is not familiar with the area. It would be very kind of you"
"You can ride with us" said the lady on the chestnut Arab "But you will have to keep up"
"Not a problem" I assured her "we will just tag along behind you, you don't need to worry about us at all".

Walking towards the mounting block I had a quick chat in Puddings rather sleepy ear 'this is a tough gig my friend, we are going to have to take it up a pace or we will get left behind. You with me'. He continued to stare at me with his eyes half open, but I am sure he understood. Once we were on our way the introductions began. I was riding with Jackie and Mandy, both very experienced long-distance riders with spritely Arab horses who seemed to float along. Pudding, with hooves like dinner plates, took a lot longer to cover the same amount of ground so we were already at a disadvantage.

The first mile or so was taken at a pace we could cope with; the ground was icy underfoot in many places, so we were cautiously picking our way along, not wanting to slip. By ten o'clock the sun was out, and the ice was melting, so the pace picked up; Pudding and I kept finding ourselves quite some distance behind our leaders and in constant trot to try and catch up. There was a point when they disappeared completely out of view and Pudding began to let out a series of whinnies, he must have felt as worried as I was – I had left the route instructions in the van and I didn't have the remotest clue where we were. We eventually caught up when they had stopped to discuss which of the various gates in front of them was the intended one for this ride. From that point I decided that even if it meant cantering, I was going to keep them in my eye line.

After a short while Mandy pulled next to me for a little chat, she was interested to know more about my riding history and was amazed when I told her that I had only been riding for two years and had owned Pudding for just over twelve months

"You're very brave coming out on your own like this" she said

"Thank you, but I'm not on my own" I grinned "I'm with you"

She laughed and told me a little more of her story, she had been riding for years and her greatest achievement was a one-hundred-mile endurance ride over several days. After my riding holiday, when fatigue set in by day three, I could not imagine how you would possibly ride that far

"You have to build up to it for months. You have to be fit and so does your horse"

I took a moment to watch her ride and was fascinated that she seemed to spend most of her time sat up balanced on her stirrups and not sat in the saddle

"It's less pressure on the horse" she smiled.

I was in awe. We had been riding for two hours and I was beginning to feel a little tired. Yet here she was, crouched in position without the slightest sign of fatigue. Wow!

We both heard Jackie ahead of us "There's a gate" she shouted.

Gathering together we approached the gate and Jackie invited me to go first. I approached from this angle and that, but just couldn't get Pudding into the right position to move forward before the gate swung shut. Mandy tried and got through in one go. Jackie tried and had as much difficulty as me, so she jumped off landing in a deep squelchy ditch of mud. I could hear her growl quietly, grabbing her Arab she remained in the same spot and swung the mare through the gate. Her feet were now rooted in the mud, so she let go of the reins and the mare trotted off down the lane.

"You might as well come through" she said, so I wasted no time in getting through the gate as instructed.
With one almighty pull she managed to break the suction and lift one boot, then the other out of the mud and wade down the path to collect her horse.

Pudding was now wide awake and had found his stride. As the ladies made off down the track he was right behind doing a steady canter, with the sound of the frost covered soil crunching beneath his hooves.

We entered a field with an ascent to the top clearly marked, so we gathered our reins and in the wintery sunshine cantered to the top. Pudding decided it was clearly a race which he had to win and put a good spurt on, his breath visible in clouds around his nose, while I applied equal amounts of effort to hold him back; I cannot imagine that crashing through my two companions would have gone down well at all. Oh, the joys of owning a boy racer.

On we went, past farms, through villages and down tracks and paths galore. We must have done around ten miles and whilst Pudding seemed fine, I was beginning to wilt. My legs ached but the real pain was elsewhere. I was chafing where no person ever wants chafing. I squirmed around in my saddle trying to find a different position to get some relief, but nothing helped. Feeling desperately sore I decided I needed to say something

"Have we got much further to go?" I gasped "Because I have serious chafing"

"Swedish Riding Knickers" returned Jackie

"Swedish Riding Knickers?" I repeated

"Swedish Riding Knickers. They provide all the protection you need. Game-changer" she replied.

I sat in the saddle absorbing this new piece of information

"I'm fine with M&S" whispered Mandy.

She probably was, as her derriere rarely touched the saddle.

The last four miles were tortuous. They were the longest four miles I have ever ridden. There was no let-up in pace and every step seemed to inflame my situation. I certainly did not want to spoil their ride, or seem like the small child on the backseat of the car, but every fifteen minutes brought another desperate plea 'Have we got much further?'

Eventually, we turned into the final road and approached the farm where we had parked. We turned into the drive and both ladies jumped off; I however needed to negotiate a very careful dismount. With tears in my eyes, I dropped the top of my body onto Puddings neck, dragged my leg over his back and slid off. This was agony. Whatever it took, I was going to find some Swedish Riding Knickers as soon as I got back.

Jackie popped round to the van just before I left

"It might be worth getting your saddle checked" she observed "I think it's probably the reason you are struggling to sit back"

I thanked her and resolved to do just that.

It was a slow and steady drive back to the yard and by the time I had unpacked everything, I went to say goodbye to Pudding only to find him in his stable looking pretty much as I had found him this morning. Half asleep, with his bottom lip drooping towards the floor.

A day or two later I was telling Kathy about Swedish Riding Knickers and she informed me that she had a pair of padded equestrian knickers I could have. She had ordered them, but they were not the style she wanted and had intended to send them back. If I wanted them, I could have them. Hell Yes! It's not often that you get the chance to wear someone else's knickers, but I have been so honoured. They are from Equestrian Derriere, with soft foamy padding right where you need it. You may walk as though you are wearing a nappy, but boy, when I wore them on the next long ride my bottom remained in a blissful cushion of happiness to the very end. God bless her!

Back to my saddle dilemma - after a few enquiries I discovered Cheshire Saddle Exchange and made an appointment for them to come and see me. There was a history with saddles and I was very reluctant to spend another small fortune on a new one. Pudding had come with tack, but the whilst the saddle was a good make it was suitable for a teenager and not a grown up with a much wider spread. I had already had Pudding checked out and he was simply built with one shoulder larger than the other, there was nothing physically wrong with him, it was nature. But I had spent the first few months extremely frustrated that the saddle constantly slipped to the side, I would need to find a way to compensate.

Acting on a recommendation I contacted a company who specialise in treeless saddles which 'mould to the shape of your horse'. Their recommended saddle fitter arrived and commenced with measuring Pudding. Quite apart from the fact that she treated the irregularity in his shape as something with worrying undertones, she assured me that the new saddle would be perfect for him. Seven weeks and a small fortune later, I now possessed a brand new purpose- built saddle. So you can imagine my disappointment when this thing still slipped to the side. After a constant roundabout of re-flocking, gel pads, gel numnahs and re-flocking, I found myself resigned to the fact that there would always be some movement and I should try and concentrate on being a 'balanced' rider; as the fitter had strongly advised that this was the root cause of the problem.

It was nearly twelve months later when I was out riding with Kathy when things came to a head. She kept observing the saddle move at the back, to the point when it was resting on Puddings spine "this is not right, you need to do something about it" she advised.

We decided to take a closer look, so making a date I hacked round to her yard where we began investigations. With just the saddle on his back, it was clear to see that at least half of it seemed to be lifting at the back and was making no contact at all. When I climbed on, it would move round and continue to do so.

"let me try it" she said and promptly got on.

After a few circuits up and down the driveway she declared that there was something wrong with it, it just 'feels wrong'. We also noticed that her left leg was stuck out slightly like mine normally does

"I just can't get into the right position in this saddle " she remarked "it's knocking my foot out".

After some more discussion we decided that I should try her saddle and I got on board her horse for a walk around. There was an epiphany moment; this saddle was firm and felt supremely comfortable. Furthermore, I could sit back properly, and my legs naturally fell into the right position.

"I thought you needed to work on your legs' she said "but it's not you at all. It's this saddle".

As you can imagine, I was furious that I spent so much money and laboured for so long with such an inferior saddle. I resolved that I would sort it out straight away, so a week later there I was with the saddle fitter from Cheshire Exchange who looked horrified at what was before her. She took me through one point after another, showing me how badly fitting my current saddle was and the damage it was doing to Pudding. His shoulder had grown considerably more in size as he was trying to compensate for the adverse pressure the saddle was placing on him. I was heartbroken and distressed that I had in any way been responsible for this. Sensing we needed to move forward quickly, she brought one saddle after another out until we found a perfect fit, an immaculate black Barnsby, which sat perfectly on his back. We made our way over to the ménage to try it out and within seconds of getting on Pudding was moving with a greater pace and ease than I had experienced before. He hates circles, but today he circled happily and stretched his legs out as though he had discovered the joy of movement for the first time. To my amazement I found that I could sit back properly and there was no need for me to try and rotate my hip round to stop my leg from sticking out. They just naturally fell to the side and we floated along together in gloriously balanced unison.

I thought I was going to cry with happiness, this was bliss. Obviously, there were a few more checks to do, but each one confirmed that this was one really well-fitting saddle. The joy did not end there, I was stunned that she would take my old saddle in exchange, so it would cost me a less than one hundred pounds to acquire this gorgeous replacement.

There is a part of me that is cross that both Pudding and I have struggled on, with both of us experiencing painful rides and sore body parts, because I had placed my trust in people who abused it. I guess I have learned a big lesson, do your research and ask around before you part with your money; and if anyone asks me what I think of the previous saddle company I will have no hesitation in telling them.

Chapter Thirteen

There are moments which you know are milestones and one was approaching. Janet and I had signed up for a charity ride to raise money for the funeral costs of a young boy who had met a sudden and tragic end. It was all very last minute, but it was relatively local, so we felt we could give it a go.

Tally Ho

There was the usual excitement in the van on the way there and also the apprehension. This was the first time we had ridden 'en-masse' and we had no idea how the horses would behave.

Janet had bought a new pair of jodhpurs for the occasion, black with a florescent stripe down the leg to match her florescent gislet.

"What do you think" she grinned "do you think people will be able to see me?"

"Well, I opened Google Earth and before I even typed in an address I could see you" I laughed in return.

As we pulled into the car park of the designated pub only a few horseboxes were there, so we quickly selected our spot, parked up and unloaded. I had no sooner got Pudding out of the van and tied up, then more horses arrived, and he decided that everything needed his fullest attention. I had the saddle on and was trying desperately to fasten the girth strap on a constantly moving horse. Ten, fifteen minutes and more passed and I was still frantically trying to get the thing secured, every time I got the strap through the buckle, he would move, and I would lose grip and need to start again. By now nearly all the horses were assembled and there was the gentle background noise of people greeting each other and exchanging pleasantries. The car park was relatively small, so most people had an excellent view of my frantic efforts and some watched me cautiously from the side of their eye while they chatted.

To my utter relief, and everyone else's, the thing was finally secured, so I whipped the small steps out of the van and tried to mount. Pudding was ready for action and would not stand still long enough for me to get on. By now, every single person in the car park was stood waiting to commence and watching me making numerous attempts to get on. This was unbearable, I decided to make use of the small wall at the side of the car park and marched Pudding over, stood on the wall and after a further three attempts I finally made a jump for it and got on board.

The organiser now exhaled and felt she could start proceedings. She welcomed us all to the ride and several helpers appeared with small glasses of port on trays and steadily made their way around the car park allowing each rider to take a glass. As I had not yet managed to get Pudding to stand still, I did grab a glass as we passed a tray and we continued to grapple together for a good few minutes as I tried to drink, and Pudding tried to mingle. Being surrounded by more than thirty horses was revving Pudding up in a way I had not seen before, he must have thought he was off hunting and we literally wrestled through the whole of the organisers speech as she dedicated the ride to the young man, with every other horse and rider quiet in solemn reflection while Pudding and I pushing our way through this horse and that. I deployed all my usual instructions and a few ad hoc ones, but he was completely ignoring me. The ride was declared open and within a split second every horse in the car park turned and made a speedy manoeuvre away from me, as though I was some giant cat that had been dropped in the centre of a colony of mice.

Janet, as supportive as ever, sat waiting at the car park entrance and gave a smile as I joined her

"well that was something else" I exclaimed "I feel like the village pariah"

We laughed as we found ourselves being propelled along by two excited horses and within minutes we had worked our way up to the centre of the pack. It was an amazing experience to be part of a large body of riders. We stretched along the road for nearly quarter of a mile with the clatter of the metal shoes on the tarmac and motorists suddenly jumping up behind their steering wheels as they turned the bend on this country road and found themselves facing a seemingly endless line of bouncing, energetic horses. There was quite a line of cars behind us when we eventually pulled off onto a track and continued on our way.

By now both our horses had calmed down and it was a great opportunity to catch up with a few people I knew and get to know a few who were new faces. There was a general air of fun in the group as we all relaxed into the ride. Our track was a small private road on which some truly beautiful and characterful houses were situated. Being the nosey soul that I am, it was a huge bonus to have some inspiring cottage renovations and dramatic gardens to enjoy. I could have quite happily continued along like that for the rest of the ride, but we turned again onto a bridleway and then the lead horse stopped at the front and announced that we were now going to have a canter, so anyone not wanting to do so should wait at the back with his colleague.

Janet was pretty adamant that she was not going, so I reluctantly said goodbye and trotted on with the rest of the group. Pudding was not initially happy at leaving Ebony, he kept trying to turn back to her as it must have seemed unusual that he was leaving her behind. We trotted on for a few minutes then turned onto a single track with the pace beginning to quicken. Within a few moments the horse in front of me was off in canter and we followed in a slow and steady fashion. This was a pleasant and collected pace and Pudding was a darling to ride, so much so, that I was sad when it came to an end. We all piled through the opening at the end of the track and gathered in a group around our lead horse. After much discussion on his phone, he rang off and announced that we would not be continuing on the planned route as Cheshire Hunt were out in the area we were heading towards and he didn't want any accidents. That absolutely fine by me. I had and still have no desire to ever get involved with a hunt.

After a few minutes we were joined by the second group who had walked along the canter track and they were informed of the change to plans. Pudding was reunited with Ebony, who was not as bothered to see him as he was to see her. Janet and I chatted as we waited to find out what was happening next

"I am afraid we will have to go back' declared the ride leader "there is no other route I can use which won't involve running into the hunt"

The general consensus was one of disappointed resignation, no one wanted to go back but equally, no one wanted to run into a pack of bloodhounds and galloping horses.

"So, who would like a canter back?" he asked

I looked at Janet

"Come on, you can do it. Just tell him you need to be in the front"

"I don't know" she replied

"I promise you it wasn't fast, and you can always tell him you need to go slowly" I returned

"But you know what she's like, she will want to race" said Janet with a furrowed brow "Blow it, go on – I will"

We edged our way to the front and asked politely if Janet could go directly behind him and could we go at a steady pace

"Sure, no problem" came the reply.

We formed a new line with Janet right behind the lead horse and made our way back onto the track. Within a couple of minutes, he had signalled we were going into canter, and nudged his horse on. For the first few minutes we made slow and steady strides, then Ebony stuck her head forward and off she went. With Janet trying desperately to pull her back, she bombed past the lead and in a blur of speed disappeared down the track. I watched helplessly as I saw the faint glow of Janet's high viz recede down the hill and out of sight. Pudding felt the race was on, pulling him back from trying to overtake in an attempt to catch Ebony nearly ragged my arms out of their sockets. The general pace had picked up, but it still felt like an age before we rounded the final bend and the end of the track was in view.

As we approached I could see Janet with flushed cheeks and wide eyes, thankfully still sat on-board a now stationary Ebony. I shouted out

"Are you OK?"

"I'm fine" she smiled.

I had expected that Janet would be shaken up, but she was calm and did not seem anywhere near as bothered as I thought she would be. Maybe she had done that much cantering at Kelsall, that today's dash didn't make that much of a mark. I was very impressed, she had clearly pushed her way out of her comfort zone in quite a spectacular fashion.

The whole ride gathered together, and we began to head back the way we came. Janet and I slotted into the line of riders and happily trotted for a couple of miles towards the pub and our waiting van. By the time we arrived back, the car park was pretty full. This was a very popular pub and their relatively meagre car park was now dominated by horseboxes and trailers. Starving motorists had stuffed their cars into every conceivable space, leaving most of us with some pretty nifty manoeuvring to get our vehicles out. This was one occasion when I was really thankfully to have a small nippy van, I knew I had just a few backwards and forwards adjustments and I would be able to get out.

We loaded the horses and decided not to leave straight away but to stay for a quick bite to eat. An estate car had appeared with several Tupperware boxes full of sandwiches and cake. We were handed a paper napkin and told to help ourselves, so we grabbed a selection of cheese, ham and salad, sat in the van and devoured them in minutes. After a plastic cup full of coffee, we felt able to make the journey home, so we said our goodbye's and buckled up.

"We did well today" I mused in the van "that was quite a big step for us"

"I feel quite proud of myself. I thought I would be too worried to do a ride like this" replied Janet "but it was fine, and I did it"

"You nailed it. And you did a canter" I said grinning

"I know" Janet giggled "The Black Blur strikes again".

It was a few days after the ride when an email from Janet pinged in my inbox. 'Check this out, it looks fabulous'. I clicked on the link and it was another charity ride. It promised fields, woodland and lots of beautiful places to enjoy a lovely canter. The clincher was the last sentence 'there will be a stop for tea and homemade cake on the way and a hot meal at the end'. I responded within a heartbeat 'book it'.

Buoyed on by the success of our last charity ride we found ourselves in the van on our way to the next one. This was another trip to the Peak District and after twenty minutes I was reliving the terror of driving through this vehicle adverse terrain. One steep hill and hairpin bend after another with a sat nav whose sole purpose was to guide me down dirt tracks and up sheer hill climbs. There was the odd moment when it would point you in one direction and then suddenly the arrow on the screen would switch to now pointing towards the turning you had just missed. It was such an action which led to one of the most terrifying driving moments I had experienced to date. We approached a corner and the arrow pointed to a spur on the right of the road, this was a single lane flanked by stone walls which made its was directly up a hill. I stopped at the turn and waited to see if the arrow moved, it didn't.

Anyone for port?

"Can this be right?" I said to Janet "it wants me to go up there"

We sat and pondered on what to do. I inched forwards and the arrow remained firmly pointing to the turn, so I made it and began to climb the hill. Within ten seconds the screen flickered, and the arrow moved back to the road we had just left. I screamed at it

"You stupid useless piece of crap"

as I suddenly felt the lurch of terror at what I now had to do.

"OMG, I will have to reverse down a hill with two horses in the back" tears now forming.

Janet jumped into leadership mode

"It will be fine, just take your time and I will jump out and direct you" to which she promptly exited the van.

With every muscle in my body tensed and my foot firmly attached to the brake, I began to reverse. We made our way steadily back down the track until we were at the junction. It never ceased to amaze me how a deserted country road suddenly fills with traffic whenever you have a difficult manoeuvre to perform. Janet took charge, marched out into the road and stopped every car in its tracks. She then signalled for me to reverse out, thanked drivers with a polite wave and jumped back into the cab with a breezy air of indifference.

"There we go" she said smiling.

"Get you!" I replied "that was brilliant. I love it when you're masterful"

After just under an hour travelling we finally turned into the mile-long driveway of the stately home hosting the ride. There were horses and trailers everywhere. We approached the entry point and two ushers signalled for us to stop.

"Can I have your names please" said one, staring at her clipboard

I gave her our names and she ticked us off her list. We were given coloured tabards, a set of instructions and told 'park over there' which was accompanied by a vague arm wave in the direction of the house. We crept through the main gates, found an opening on the grass under a tree and parked up.

In no time at all we were tacked up and off, it looked amazing, with undulating fields and forests wherever you looked. We went through the first set of gates and the usher greeted us

"Do you want to use the warm up field or go directly onto the ride" she enquired

"Directly onto the ride" we replied

"In that case you make your way through the far gate " she said waving her hand in the general direction we should travel "and follow the arrows from there"

This was so exciting, we made our way down the track, through the gate and into the field turning sharp left as directed by our first sign. We potted on alongside a wall, made our way to the corner where both horses decided that we would go wide to avoid any contact with the field of bulls on the other side. The wall ended, and our arrow directed us to continue along the next fence line.

If there had not been so many arrows we would have thought that we were in the wrong field. We now found ourselves suddenly picking our way along the track at the top of a steeply sloping hill.

"Where does this go?" asked Janet "surely we don't have to go down there"

We got to the next wall and the track turned and sure enough we were staring at steep descent for the full width of the field.

"You've got to be kidding me" I gasped

With resignation we sat back in our saddles as both ponies slowly shuffled their way down. There was a beautiful view of the lake, but that was pretty much the only thing to commend it so far. We turned at the bottom and followed the arrows on the same track, until we were eventually at the end and making our ascent back up the hill.

"that looks promising" I observed, pointing towards the grey slate farm estate "maybe we are going up through there"

Within minutes the track led us straight back to the gate we had used when we first entered the field. We had basically done one big circle. This was the point that it began to dawn on us that this was perhaps not going to be the ride we were promised. Indeed, this ride would end up being anything but the one we expected.

Through the gate we were greeted by another usher who informed us that we should make our way around the next field, but would we mind staying in walk as there was a mare with foal in the adjacent field and they did not want to frighten them with horses cantering past. We both stared blankly. But being British and not wanting to offend, we ended up thanking him and proceeding on our way. One steady walk around the next field we were back at the gate again and this time directed to cross the road. We made our way down the estate driveway and out through the gates, to find several ushers in charge of traffic management. They politely stopped the cars and we trotted on down the short section of road and through the next set of estate gates. The next section was magical, as we had magnificent houses and gardens to look at and admire. We engaged in endless chatter and giggles about who might live there and how we would make much better occupants. Within no time at all the driveway came to an end and we were at a T junction with a road. There was not one single arrow or usher.

"Where do we go now? When you are in a field there are a hundred arrows but get to a T junction and there's not a single one" I observed.

"It could be either way" replied Janet "I've no idea".

We sat for a moment considering our options, when we heard the sound of horses approaching

"thank goodness, we can ask them" I said

We were informed of the direction and made our turn watching them trot off into the distance. The road was a typically beautiful country lane, with cottages and smallholdings dotted along the route. We chatted and walked, generally enjoying being out in such glorious surroundings. It was roughly twenty minutes later when we finally made our way into a local village of breath-taking beauty. It was also then that we realised the traffic had increased quite considerably and we were now wearing only the tabards provided by the ride organisers and not our usual high viz

"I don't feel at all comfortable being out on the road without it" came Janet's concerned voice from behind me

"Me neither" I replied

This was a point on which I felt quite strongly. You shouldn't take risks when you are out on the road, you are putting the lives of motorists, your horse and yourself in danger when you cannot be seen.

Feeling on edge we plodded through the village and out on to another equally busy road, hoping that we were going in the right direction. After a few metres an arrow finally appeared and indicted that we should be veering to the left down a side track. We were very thankful to finally be off the main road and began to relax as soon as we were safely on the dirt path. To either side of us there were slate buildings, so old and small that you could touch the roof. We could see the turning on the track ahead, with two riders approaching, they levelled with us and told us a piece of information which brightened things considerably – just one hundred yards along was the stop for cake and tea. And furthermore, the cake was delicious. This is what we had been looking forward to, so we thanked them profusely and the thought of cake must somehow have fogged the brain, as the final comment 'watch out for the pigs' went pretty much unnoticed.

We turned the bend and the track dropped down, leaving the old stone wall raised above us. Pudding was happily leading the way, as we progressed chatting gaily about cake. Without warning two pigs darted up from behind the wall, their heads directly level with Pudding's and screeched for all they were worth. Pudding jumped in the air, spun round and made a bolt back down the track, his progress only hindered by Ebony who was herself in the process of trying to turn at speed. The sudden spin had dislodged me, and I was propelled forward with one foot out of the stirrup and to my dismay both horses now picked up pace and were bolting down the track towards the road. In those moments as we hurtled forwards, I was desperately trying to regroup and managed to get back into position in the saddle, with my foot flailing wildly in search of the stirrup. Pulling for all we were worth, we finally got them into a trot as we swung off the track and back onto the road, there was no way they were stopping, so the best we could do was keep them in trot until some of their energy had been diffused. We bounced along, with two jumpy and anxious horses for quite some way. Even when we did slow the pace slightly, Pudding was still very jumpy, and I could not get him to step down from the joggy walk he had adopted. We had already turned off the busy road onto a quieter lane riding two agitated horses.

There was no fury in an exchange like the one we engaged in for the following few minutes. Who the hell would organise a ride where it was possible for pigs to jump out and ambush your horse? Quite frankly, had the horses made a sharper turn we could have come off with any number of scenarios. There was the possibility of hitting our heads on the wall, getting trampled underfoot, horses bolting off into cars and any other number of possibilities. It was the most stupid piece of planning I think I had ever encountered.

But our afternoon was to continue in much the same vein. Within a few minutes we were joined by a group of riders, who quickly had us surrounded. Enveloped in this bunch of horses we proceeded down the lane together until we approached a field with thirty or more horses directly on the other side of the small slate wall. Having heard the clatter of hooves approaching they were now galloping wildly around their field, turning to gallop towards us just as we were passing. Pudding stopped dead and froze with fear. The first half of the group scuttled about on the road and then moved quickly on, while the second half were now stuck behind the motionless Pudding. His eyes were transfixed on the galloping group as he tried to get to grips with what was happening.

"I say" said a rather haughty rider from behind us "can you move on"

Janet took the lead and nudged Ebony forwards, which seemed to snap Pudding out of his trance and into his next panic – where had all the horses in front of him gone? For the second time he was clearly distressed and jogged along trying to catch up with the group in front, while I found myself stuck in some no man's land miles ahead of Ebony yet still miles behind the lead group. I tried to get him to stop but he wouldn't stand still, so eventually I deployed my old faithful and did circles until Janet and the others caught up. Janet was relieved to be back with me, as the haughty lady had been passing remarks about us and Janet was just about ready to explode with a few remarks of her own.

"Well I am going off down the detour for a canter " exclaimed haughty, to which she and her friend made a speedy departure.

"She was driving me nuts" declared Janet "I swear if she had said one more thing..."

For the second time that day we 'vented' our feelings while I did circles around Janet, as Pudding was still not ready to stand still. The sign next to us indicated that we could detour off for five miles through the woods or follow the arrows along the main route back towards the hall. At this point I could not imagine what would happen if I asked Pudding to canter; judging by his current mood it would probably consist of a bolt from one end of Derbyshire to the other. We decided that we really did not trust the organisation of this ride one jot and that our safest bet would be to continue back to the van. We continued along the road and were alarmed to find that we were almost immediately back at the road being ushered back across into the hall grounds. We made our way back up the long driveway with sinking disappointment, after all the anticipation this ride had proved to be a complete disaster.

Pudding was still not settled and full of energy when we got to the van and even after I had tied him up, he swung from one side to the other jumping on the spot. He had not yet had anywhere to release his energy and it was all bottled up, needing to go somewhere. We were done. Tack was off and packed up and he needed to be loaded – but he was not ready to quit yet. It took four of us to get him into the van, where he shuffled about restlessly for the following half an hour.

My phone rang and one of the organisers was concerned that we had missed all of the checkpoints since leaving the hall grounds. I just about held my temper as I grunted 'pigs', 'bolt' and other random words down the phone, to which she exclaimed 'then you must have a full refund'. I hung up and Janet said she would go and try to explain what had happened to us. She returned a short while later and said that the organiser was very apologetic, it was the first ride she had organised and had not thought about high visibility clothes or the proximity of the pigs. I did soften at this point, she had clearly tried to do a good thing to raise funds for charity, but I couldn't help feeling that she could have asked for some advice from more experienced ride organisers – as this had proved to be one I would never forget, for all the wrong reasons.

Once the engine was running and we were pulling out of the driveway, I decided that I would detour round to the motorway as I was really not in the mood to take on the battle between Peak District roads and my sat nav. It was three and half exhausting hours later before we finally pulled into the yard.

Lows in the Peaks

A week or so later and feeling rather disgruntled about organised rides, I was delighted to get an email from Jackie to say that she would be happy to take me around Delamere if I fancied it, as she lived locally and knew the forest well. She finished the email with a killer hook 'I know lots of routes people know nothing about'.

'I'm in' I replied.

Kathy was keen to join, so we arranged a date and time - everything was set. The only thing you can't predict is the weather. For the few days before there had been gale force winds and heavy rainstorms and the weather app showed that we were in for some forceful blasts and heavy showers on the day of the ride. At this point I had not been out on Pudding for a proper hack for nearly two weeks, so I was determined to go. To my great relief Kathy felt the same way, so we rendezvoused at the car park and following Jackie on her fast Arab off we went.

I had left the yard that morning to a series of lifted eyebrows and a few 'I wouldn't chance it today' comments, but to my absolute delight, there was no wind and the sun shone. I have no idea what weather the app was predicting, but it was perfect riding weather in Delamere.

We set off at pace and within a few minutes Jackie was suggesting a canter. Now up to this point I had thought Pudding could shift, but he was outclassed by the Arab who seemed to have completed the canter stretch before we had even got going. Kathy's Connemara could also move and was not far behind the leader. But I will give Pudding his due, by the end of the next canter he had lifted his game and whilst he was still a resounding third, the margin had greatly decreased.

We spent the next few hours darting through one track and then another, onto paths then back into little lines through the undergrowth only to emerge moments later onto another well marked path. I marvelled at Jackie's comprehensive knowledge of the forest and the ease with which she traversed it. Whichever way we wanted to go, she had multiple ways of getting there and it was fun to just relax and let her lead us.

Our final canter down the path towards the car park was by far the fastest. Pudding picked up speed after a few minutes and we were bombing along, with the foliage beside us a complete blur. About half way along it struck me just how fast we were going and how horrible it would be to fall off, but one thing I have learned is that minute you let fear take over, you make mistakes, panic, act stupidly and put yourself in danger. I had a quick talk to myself, told myself to grab his mane for extra safety and RIDE it. So that is what I did, feeling totally exhilarated when we finally came to a halt.

Once back at the yard it was sheeting down, and I got utterly drenched just walking the short distance from the van to the stable with Pudding. One or two liveries came for a chat and I am not sure anyone believed me when I said that we had enjoyed great weather at Delamere, as apparently it had been like that all day back at the yard.

I reflect on that ride as one I utterly enjoyed and to add to my happiness the camera worked, so it is something I can replay in the quiet of the evening when I just want to remind myself that I actually did it.

Chapter Fourteen

The next few weeks ended up being a huge roller coaster, as I moved livery yards, it all happened quite quickly. It was not just about moving a horse, but a real departure, the end of an era. The winter months had taken their toll; the long commute to and from the yard twice a day seemed to affect everything, there was little time to get anything else done other than the horse duties. On top of that, there were fewer and fewer people turning their horses out in the fields when they were based in paddocks across the road, so there were many days when the weather was fine, but Pudding found himself stuck in a stable because I could not leave him in his field on his own, with no other horse in sight.

One evening I sat talking to Phil at length about the whole situation and it seemed pretty clear at the end of it, that I should try and find a yard closer to home with regular turnout for Pudding. After weeks of being churned up about the situation, now having a clear course of action suddenly settled me and I began the search for the best place to move to.

Obviously, I wanted somewhere closer to home, so I arranged to visit a large livery only 4 miles from my house. After several texts it was set up for me to meet Alistair at 11am the following morning. Arriving at the time agreed, I pulled into the car park to be greeted by a tall spindly man with a generally happy and self-deprecating manner.

"I'm just a farmer" he confided "but our family have been here for four hundred years"

You could tell the pride he held for the place and so he should, it was absolutely immaculate. There were two Martin Collins arenas which any livery could freely use, a field with jumps in, a canter field, separate paddocks for each horse and then there were the stables. Two huge barns with large airy stables and so much room, you could tie your horse up outside your stable and still access all everything you needed in the centre aisle. I had my only private alarmed locker room and it was set up for part livery; they would put Pudding in his field in the morning, bring him back, muck out, change rugs and hang his hay net up. I was overwhelmed, this was fabulous. And as an extra Brucey Bonus the exit from the farm led onto the bridlepath no more than five minutes ride from Kathy's.

Alistair was enjoying his role as tour guide and ran through every particular in great detail. He even showed me the hay barn and explained the qualities of the various ears of hay poking their way out of the bales.

In the centre of the hay barn were two immaculate red tractors

"I've never been in a tractor" I remarked

No sooner had I said this, when I found myself being escorted to the nearest one, hoisted in and shown all the controls. On a roll I asked if I could move the large scoop at the front, so the engine was switched on and I spent a few happy minutes twiddling the knob and watching the large arms move up and down.

Tractors are quite a piece of kit. This one had Bluetooth, radio, heated seats, full surround view camera and a whole heap more gadgets which I have since forgotten. I no longer feel any pity for farmers out tending fields in all weathers, believe me, it's party time in that cab.

My final request was to walk down the track which led to the back of the farm to view the canter field and exit to the bridlepath.

"Not a problem" smiled Alistair.

I set off walking, but within minutes Alistair and his quad bike had pulled next to me

"Hop on the front" he shouted

I stared at the small rack of bars on the front in horror. Really? Not wanted to appear rude, I jumped on and off we sped. I could see the accelerator handle from the corner of my eye and we seemed to be turned onto full throttle. Down the gravel path we flew, while I hung onto the bars beneath me with every ounce of strength I possessed. Ahead I could see the field, I full expected that we would stop, but no. We bounced onto the grass and continued at break neck speed with me bouncing around like a pea on a drum. Suddenly Alistair's head shot forward next to mine

"Nearly there" he observed.

We stopped abruptly, and I jumped off.

"I'll just have a look around then and meet you back at the stable block"

"Oh, don't you worry. Take as long as you like, then I can run you back" replied Alistair

"No, no, it's alright. I can quite happily walk" I replied in desperation.

But he sat back on his seat and I resigned myself to the fact that I was returning across the green mile again perched on the front of the quad. We flew back at the same speed with which we travelled out and it took me a few minutes to feel fully co-ordinated when I was finally stood back on solid ground.

After a short discussion about charges and facilities I decided that this was going to be a great place to come and agreed there and then that I would move.

As I drove home I thought about the yard I was departing and there was a sadness at leaving so many dear friends and such a mountain of happy memories. That was a period in time which is etched on my heart forever; a time of laughter, adventure, friendship and discovery. I will always look back on my time there as some of the happiest and I am thankful for the ladies who helped make it that way.

But here I was about to embark on another new adventure, so fast forward four weeks and I am now driving into my new yard with Pudding in the van and wondering how he was going to feel about everything. It had been bitterly cold, the Beast from the East had brought sub-zero temperatures, so Pudding had spent most of the week before in his stable. He exited the van and walked with me down the gravelly path to his paddock where I let him loose. I had expected that he would do a canter round or at least have a good sniff, but overwhelmed by the fact there was grass, he dropped his head and just stood there munching. All his paddock neighbours stood to attention waiting to say hello, but they gave up hope after fifteen minutes when there was no sign that the new boy was going to raise his head and actually acknowledge them.

I finished unloading my things, went to check on Pudding who was still eating, then drove home. There was a real sense of a weight being lifted. I didn't have to go back to bring him in, but I couldn't settle until I had been back and checked on him and obviously had a cuddle. The following day, which just happened to be a Saturday, Phil and I stayed in our PJs until 3pm, watching TV and generally behaving like fresher students. The following week I really could not believe how easy things were. I went down once a day to check he was Ok and to muck out anything that needed shifting before he went to bed.

By the second week I began to feel a little uneasy. The time Pudding was spending in his paddock was quite limited; he was out at 6am and back in his stable for 11am. His paddock was covered in skid marks (used in the correct context here), telling me that he was constantly feeling startled and making a run for it. And now he was spending more time than ever in his stable, nearly nineteen hours out of every twenty-four.

By week three his temperament began to change, little subtle things. He was so much more spookier and alarmed by things. He was clingy and did not want me to go. He just seemed depressed.

The weather was the worst I had ever seen it, with temperatures dropping to minus 5 and below. I would fill the water bucket only to see the ice crystals form right in front of my eyes. I literally had to take a hammer to it to break the four inches of solid ice which had formed by the morning. All the liveries banded together to try and help each other out, but the place did not have the same heartbeat as my last one. People were very pleasant but there was a sense of fear constantly hanging in the air. It didn't take long for me to understand why.

"Alistair has a terrible temper on him" confided one lady "and it can be for the slightest thing"
"Really? He seemed very nice to me" I replied
"Oh, he can be, but then he can just turn. And when he does he can kick you off the yard"
"Really?" I replied, like a stuck record
"Yes, he will usually tell you that you have two hours to get your things packed and go".

I now began to feel the same sense of anxiety, as though the axe may fall at any moment. The general consensus was that you need to keep your head down and try not to get noticed. Ok, understood.

The weather was not getting any better, in fact it had been so bad that the paths to the paddocks were too icy for the horses to walk on, so they had been stuck inside for days. I decided that Pudding needed to get out, so I walked him into the ménage and let him off his lead rope, as I had done many times at my old yard. He was ecstatic to finally get a chance to stretch his legs and went for a full gallop all the way around, accompanied by some flamboyant bucks. After several circuits he stopped dead, dropped to his knees and began the longest roll ever.

It was at this point I could see Barbara running towards me at break neck speed waving her arms
"Don't let Alistair see you" she shouted as she approached "quick, get him back on the lead rope"
"Why, what's wrong?"
"You are not allowed to let them loose in here, Alistair will go mental"

We spent the next few minutes trying to discretely catch a galloping pony, only succeeding when we adopted a pincer manoeuvre and had him cornered. As we stood there panting with exhaustion we cast our eyes over the snow-covered surface of the ménage. We figured that we could comfortably explain the hoof prints around the centre, but there was nothing we could think of that would justify the large crater in the centre where Pudding had decided to take a roll. Taking a quick look around we decided that the coast was clear and high-tailed it back to the stable.

As the weeks passed I made sure I followed every rule, even the daft ones.

"You need to make sure your locker door is shut when you are not in it" observed Barbara

"Even when I am stood right next to it tacking up?" I replied

"Yes"

"But I am going backwards and forwards getting things, why do I need to keep it shut?" I continued

"Because Alistair thinks that birds fly in there and set the alarm off"

I stood looking at her with incredulity "It's a contact alarm. He even showed me the contact points on the door. It would have to be a bird carrying a crowbar to set that alarm off"

"I know" came the reply.

But the warning bells rang one evening. I had been out in the van doing a drill riding session and had returned a little later than usual, as I had dropped a friend off. As I turned onto the long driveway and neared the house I could see his outline in the shadows, he was clearly waiting for me. I drove round and parked up and he just appeared

"You know I have no one on this yard after 8pm"

"No Alistair, I didn't know that" I replied

"Oh yes you do, I clearly remember telling you when you viewed. I always tell people when I am level with that ménage over there"

Maybe he did, he told me a lot of things of that day and I simply do not remember any discussion about last times on the yard. But mindful of how things could escalate I apologised profusely and said I would be as fast as I could. He scowled and replied "well just make sure you are gone by 8"

I looked at my watch, I had three minutes to get Pudding off the van, into the stable and into my car. Moving as fast as I could I managed to do what needed to be done and got in my car for just after eight.

On the way home, I wondered if I had just been 'Alistaired'. I had been told that when you are Alistaired you get the full hairdryer treatment, whilst that was uncomfortable it certainly didn't feel like a full blast. It seemed such a shame that he was working so hard to maintain an immaculate livery yard, with Olympic standard facilities, yet people were so unhappy there. The whole place lacked any sort of heartbeat, it was soulless.

Now this is where a bit of serendipity kicked in. Kathy had told me about a lovely yard just mile further along the road which was owned by some good friends of hers. It was a small ten stable livery, full of friendly people and everyone loved being there. So much so, that places rarely became available. I had approached them when I was initially looking to move but they had no stables free. I did however get to know the owner and her friend, who did most things together. They were really genuine, totally lovely people and I thoroughly enjoyed doing any activities with them. We would laugh so much, everything felt like huge fun.

It so happened that one lady's bad fortune turned out to be my very good fortune. One of the liveries who had three horses stabled at the yard, had quite suddenly had to have one of her horses put to sleep, which meant there was now a stable free. I got a call to asking me whether I still wanted a place there and the answer was resounding yes. This gorgeous little yard is like stepping into a Darling Buds of May film set. It has none of the frills or facilities that Alistair's yard possesses but it has heart and soul in bucket loads. The whole yard join in together with so many different activities that sometimes it's a full-time job keeping track of everything that is going on. There is plenty of banter, laughter and fun. And if that was not enough in itself, Pudding adores it there. Within a day he had settled, made friends with his field mate and has become the laid back, spook free little gem I know and love. This little moorland pony who is built for life outdoors, now spends his entire day in his paddock with his new field mates.

Chapter Fifteen

On one of Sia's visits to Cheshire we went to Somerford Park, just to show her the facilities. It was a gloriously sunny day as we made our way down to the eighty-acre course and we were delighted to find there was a cross country camp that weekend and all the stables were full of horses and riders buzzing with excitement. We stood and watched one eye-catching iron grey gelding prance across the track and onto the course and for several mesmerising minutes we were all caught up in the joy of the moment, as they cantered around taking in one jump after another. I am sure we all have times when we see somebody do something and wish it was us doing it instead. That was such a moment for me, I really wanted to experience the joy of being out in the open with my own horse, just enjoying the whole adventure of it all. So when I spotted an event advertised for a three-day camp for any level of rider, based at the Somerford stables, I registered to go immediately. Back in dismal January it was something glorious to look forward to and to add to my joy, Kathy decided she would like to come too.

The week before had been an absolute scorcher, so I was pretty relieved that the forecast for our week was cooler, with the chance of showers. The plan was a simple one, you arrived at Somerford on the Sunday evening to deposit your horse in an allotted stable then returned the following morning to begin camp at 9.30am. I had spent the afternoon loading the van with everything I thought I could possibly need and when the time was right we loaded Pudding and set off. It was a warm sunny evening and as I drove down the long gravelly drive I could already see the place was alive with activity. Horseboxes and trailers were parked everywhere, in the car park and spilling out onto the grassy verges and fields. Bewildered horses were being led around and you could just see the tops of rider's heads as they staggered, laden with saddles and other various bits of kit, into the stable area. I pulled around and parked on the field, absorbing the whole atmosphere. It was like stepping back to that moment nearly two years before when I had wished I was part of it and now there was a growing feeling of excitement in the bottom of my stomach that I was actually doing this.

I jumped out of the van, opened the exit door so Pudding could stick his head out and see what was going on, while I went to find an organiser and get my instructions.

With everything set up, I led Pudding down the exit ramp and across the grass to the stable block. I was used to his avid sniffing when we went somewhere new and he certainly had plenty to sniff at today. Once deposited in his stable he stood staring at all the commotion from over his stable door while I finished unpacking all my kit. Eventually Phil arrived, and we stood together looking out over the expansive green in front of us

"Do you remember this?" I asked

"I certainly do" he replied

"I can't believe I am actually here. I'm so excited"

He smiled and replied "you enjoy it love"

After one final check on Pudding and a chat with Kathy who had now arrived, we said our goodbyes and Phil drove me home.

I was already up and dressed when the alarm clock went off and back at the stables for seven thirty. Pudding seemed a little agitated, apparently the horse next door had spent the night banging his hoof on the stable door, so I'm not sure Pudding had had much sleep. This was coupled with the fact that he was in a strange environment, full of unfamiliar smells, sounds and horses.

"Come on now baby" I assured him as I stood grooming him "it's going to be alright. Just you wait to see what we've got instore for you"

Obviously, I knew what he did not, that I had signed up for the jump clinic and I had every intention of making these three days the right of passage to very basic cross- country courses. We were starting with pole work, then jumping small cross poles and building up to 50com jumps and a chance to play on a section of the eighty-acre course.

At nine thirty I left Pudding tacked up and walked with Kathy to the pavilion for our introductory meeting. After all the introductions and housekeeping was completed, there was a general consensus that all the horses are generally very excitable on the first day and that we should all travel down the half mile track leading to the ménage areas together. There were knowing glances and chatter among the ladies who had been before, they had experienced this previously and it was something no one was looking forward to. At this point, my relaxed state was changing to one of mild disturbance. This was something that even very seasoned riders were wary of, and here I was, a complete newbie with a sleep deprived and already anxious horse.

Back at the stables ladies were already leading their horses out into the sunshine and many were mounted and stood waiting for others to join. Small groups had set off and we could see them in the distance, so without ceremony I grabbed Pudding, led him out and got on. This was the first time he had seen this huge body of horses and I felt the wave of energy shoot through him. I struggled to keep him still, so we walked around doing circles until he stopped for a few moments and then we had to repeat the whole process again. At one point a coloured cob broke loose from the rider just as she was trying to mount, and he shot off down the track. Thank fully he was quickly caught and brought back, but this was enough to energise the whole group and it moved the threat level up to Defcon 3.

I knew Pudding had hunted in the past and the sight of acres of green fields, horses everywhere and dogs barking made him as springy as I have ever known him. All I needed now was a bugle and we'd be off...

We finally got going with Pudding moving in the oddest fashion, we were walking but it was short choppy little bursts – as though we were playing a game of tag and we were trying to sneak up behind someone. It felt like I was sitting on the top of Mount Etna which was about to erupt, it was terrifying.

"Breathe, just breathe" said a lovely lady next to me "keep calm and breathe. They are always like this on the first day"

"OK" I squeaked

After what felt like a lifetime, we were finally through the gate and into the enclosed area. Now I could breathe. We were divided into our groups and thankfully our arena was at the furthest point away from all the action. The session began, lots of trotting this way and that, generally to calm everyone down and settle the horses into their new environment. We trotted over a few poles on the ground, while the instructor provided observations and generally assessed our riding ability. Before we knew it, the session was finished, and we grouped together for the walk back. Pudding had expended quite a bit of energy over the hour and a half, so he was much more relaxed on the return journey. I began to relax too, this is going to be alright after all.

Lunch was a jolly affair, with everyone sat around four long tables busy opening their lunch packs and slurping on their tea. Conversation was plentiful and there was a general sense of relief that we had all made it through the first morning unscathed. As I waited for the kettle I met two fun women and began with the banter.

We tried to exchange names and I had to confess that I have an appalling memory for names and found it helped if I could think of someone with a similar name. The first lady became Fireman Sam, which obviously prompted general banter about how 'match happy' they must be in Pontypridd, as they have so many fires. The second lady was ahead of the game and offered her university name 'Rashers'
"Because I always ate bacon butties"

They couldn't think of anyone called Caroline, so I offered Princess Caroline of Monaco, as I know this was what inspired my mother when she chose the name. I didn't think anything of it at the time.

Lunch over I went back to the stable block to find Kathy trying to figure out how to get my girth sorted. I had been telling her about 'Puffer Pudding' who would blow himself up like a puffer fish whenever I came to put the girth on. He was a size 42" but the end of the strap was literally five inches from the buckle when you first try to fasten it. You had to hold it tight for a good few minutes to fool Pudding into thinking it was fastened before you stood any chance of him breathing out, letting you get it anywhere near the buckle. Once it is fastened it goes to the second or third hole – so I know just how full of air that guy is. Kathy suddenly jerked forward in agony. Pudding had moved and trodden on her toe. She limped out

"Your horse has just trod on my toe and it *really* hurts"

I was mortified. She had gone in to help me and Bigfoot had repaid her with a horrible red and swollen toe. No amount of apologising seemed quite adequate.

We were told to get a move on as everyone was leaving, so we quickly got ready and were back down the track and into our afternoon session. I had expected Pudding to be a lot more settled, but as we began to warm up he seemed more agitated than ever. We were now in a central arena with horses all around us, jumps set up everywhere and the advanced riders in the next menage had already started their session only feet away from us. I decided to trot Pudding over a pole on the floor, but as we got close he broke into canter and jumped it. This was a whole heap more energy than I was used to, I'd normally have some serious geeing up before we got this much compulsion. As we circled around the horse in the arena next to us jumped the fence behind us and his hoof hit the plate, Pudding spooked, and all four feet left the floor, I manage to stay on for that bit but then he spun round to see what was behind him and that's when I fell off. To my absolute horror Pudding took off. He bolted out of our arena, across the grass then through all the remaining arenas, until he got to the farthest one where he eventually stopped with a group of riders.

The entire camp stopped what it was doing and stared at him as he went, officials had hands in the air shouting "Loose horse, loose horse" for all they were worth.

In the far distance I could see someone had got hold of his reins and had begun to lead him back in my direction. From nowhere the emotion of the moment caught me and I burst into tears, there was no denying I felt pretty shook up.

They led Pudding back to me and handed over the reins. Then the unthinkable happened, he took one look at my tearstained face, jerked back pulling himself free and bolted back to where they had just retrieved him. The camp had just begun to recommence with their activities and for the second time everyone froze as Pudding went charging through, with officials now well practised in the 'loose horse' shout out. I stared in disbelief, watching my little white pony go full gallop through every arena, dodging instructors and horses as he went. For the second time he was caught and led back, but this time the official was holding onto him.

"I don't like being beaten, but I think this time I am" said the instructor "I really don't think you should get back on"
"I don't want to get back on " I sobbed
"Mmm. Well perhaps you could get a lunge line for leading him back" she replied

I was so grateful that one of my friends was helping that day. She gave me an enormous hug and some soothing words of encouragement, before I turned to walk the long track back to the stable to retrieve my rope.

I was just heading back with the line when Rashers appeared with Pudding in tow.

"Here we go, one naughty pony" she grinned

We walked him back to the stable and he was still jumpy and pratting around. He was not his normal self all at, I was struggling to think of any time when I had seen him quite so agitated since those first few days when he arrived in Cheshire. We quickly got the tack off and left him in his stable to pace around.

"You need tea" said Rashers and appeared a few minutes later with a mug of steaming tea and a packet of bourbon biscuits
"Eat" she instructed "you need the sugar"

She was my hero that day, staying with me while my emotions settled and completely supportive when I found myself having another little cry. There is a certain irony in the fact that I am not a huge fan of people with overactive displays of emotion, yet today I found myself unable to stop the flood of feelings that swept through me. It was a strange release of fear, disappointment and shock. I had been looking forward to this for months and not once had I even considered that Pudding may behave badly. It had shaken me up more than I had realised.

After a while Rashers had to get back to duties, so I stayed with Pudding stroking his neck over the stable door and singing a couple of daft songs to calm him down. Something had really frightened him, he was probably completely overwhelmed, and it was just too much for him to handle. This was so unlike him, I knew it was not bad behaviour, but a response and I couldn't stay upset with him for long. Eventually he settled, and I felt comfortable enough to leave him and make some plans. It was clear to me that I couldn't leave him in the stable overnight again, he would have to go home, and I would return in the morning. So once everyone had returned and things had settled, I reversed the van to block entrance and loaded him. Once home, I stuck him straight in the field to let him have a run around and get any last tension out of his system. This was going to make the whole camp experience a much harder affair than I had planned, as it now involved an even earlier rise to get Pudding back to Somerford before the first session each morning.

I got home, and the phone pinged, it was a picture of Kathy's now black and inflamed toe. Dear god, I am not sure the day could actually have gone much worse.

Sitting quietly with a cup of tea I began to think about exactly how I was going to deal with the day's events. The whole thing had unnerved me, I was not expecting the drama to get to the arenas nor Puddings reaction to being surrounded by dozens of animated horses. I really did not want to just quit, as tempting as it truly was, but I couldn't do another day like today. I reflected on some of the things we had learnt on the NLP course and focussed on getting my mind into a positive place. Once I was feeling a little better I began to work towards a positive set of goals; calmly walking down to the arenas, being settled and quiet while we did our exercises together and a gentle relaxed walk back to the stable block. At this point I had no idea whether any of this would work, all I could say was that I was in a better place about it and determined to go back.

We returned the following morning and as we walked back into the stable block Kathy was stood waiting

"I wasn't sure you'd come" she said
"I had to' I replied "or I'd never do a camp again"

Time was tight, so I quickly tacked up and joined Kathy to walk the horses out of the stable block and into the sunlight. Once mounted Pudding stood still, we were both relaxed now he had figured out the drill. We all walked down to the arenas without incident and the first session was over in a blur. Pudding was back to his usual lazy self and unrecognisable as the pony everyone experienced yesterday

"Gosh he is so much better today" commented one lady on a large bay
"Today is he back to being Pudding" I replied "yesterday he was the devil's food cake"
She laughed, and I hoped that would be the end of it.

I am going to be honest, I was really disappointed that I had been removed from any of the jumping activities, as that was the sole reason for coming to the camp in the first place. I could understand why, but it was still frustrating, as Pudding was back to his old self today and highly unlikely to go bombing off again. But sometimes life gives you what you need instead of what you want. Under the intensive observation of our instructor I was 'worked on'. I had no idea that the little subtleties of manoeuvring a horse had escaped me. Pudding and I were hacking professionals, but under close scrutiny in the arena, we lacked the precision and control most of the other more experienced riders demonstrated with ease. I cannot recall ever working so hard, it was physically and mentally exhausting trying to co-ordinate brain and body - I knew what I wanted to do, but that was not what was happening. I would get my leg position right but one glance at my hands and you would think I was doing my knitting. By the time the session finished I was flaked and delighted to finally stop. We quietly snaked our way back to the stables and a glorious break for lunch.

As we assembled for the afternoon session the heavens opened and it started chucking it down. Finding every piece of waterproof clothing I could find, I layered up and we trooped down the arena for our next polework session. An hour and a half later I was soaked through, even my knickers were wet. But we were learning new things and improving, so it did seem worth the discomfort.

Last session over we repeated the formula which had worked well the night before, Pudding was packed up and deposited back in his own stable ready for the final day at camp.

Morning came, and we were back bright and early for our last few sessions. I had heard that I was with the group doing part of the 80 acres, but on arrival I found I had been slotted into the flatwork session. Once in the arena I did a little exercise with equitation balls. You place a special ball under your bottom and then ride and within minutes you can feel where you are unbalanced, so you spend the next few minutes rapidly learning how to correct your wobbling seat. Then we focussed on my hands, they need to be completely independent of my body, so I do not use them to balance myself and pull unnecessarily on Puddings mouth.

Pole work in the rain

"Put your hand upside down" advised my instructor
"Really?" I said, struggling to come to terms with holding the reins in a way that felt so foreign to me
"Yep, try it"

So I did. It was as though I was pushing a pram, this was weird.

"Now trot" she said waving her hand in the general direction she wished me to travel.

Tentatively I set off and to my surprise my hands did not move an inch, I couldn't ride easily, but my hands were fine.

"Practice this when you get home and it will help enormously" she smiled.

Then the more repetitive work began. Getting control by practising walk/trot transitions then trot/canter transitions. Being firm with my lazy horse, so he had one second to do as I say and staying doing it or he got a tap of the whip

"You're just too soft on him Caroline" my instructor said firmly "you need to be a lot tougher"

Tough Caroline took a little finding, I don't like using the crop and Pudding put in a little buck when we rounded a corner, he went to slow down, and I tapped him for slowing down. I guess he was no fan of the tough new me.

After an hour we were bobbing along in a grand fashion, Pudding seemed to resign himself to the fact that the game was up, and I was feeling that it was so much easier to ride a horse that kept an even pace.

Ready for lunch we all piled into the pavilion for the bring and share feast. After food was consumed we had the customary

Thank You's and handing out the rosettes. My turn arrived, and I was not surprised to get a special mention.

The organiser stood rosette in hand as I walked up "Pudding wasn't sure he wanted to be here on the first day" this was met with a round of laughter "but we are glad he changed his mind and decided to stay".

Back at my table the teasing continued

"We were using the balance balls when he ran over, so I handed the ball to my friend" grinned one lady "we had just put them back when we heard 'loose horse' and my friend said 'balls again' "

"I'm thinking of changing his name to Bernie the Bolt" I replied, knowing she was old enough to get the reference.

I am not sure why a wave of emotion hit me after lunch, as everything had been going so well for the last two days. But it did. I had been given 'the talk' on learning to control my horse and I just felt a little overwhelmed by it all. As we walked into the arena for the last session I began to feel like I wanted to go home. Our last instructor was a wily old lady, thin as a rake with a seen all-weathers face. As the other two riders took their horses off to warm up, she stood and listened as I rhymed off some lame excuse for taking Pudding back to the stable.

"well I think you should give it a go" she said, staring directly at me "I think you'll benefit from it"

She was the kind of woman who said things in a manner that did not require a response. So I sat still while she called the others back and began

"Today we are going to be doing a prelim dressage test"

You have got to be kidding me. I was already feeling a little fragile and thought of struggling to perform a prelim dressage test with three very proficient riders watching me had little appeal.

"I will break this down and we will do it one step at a time" she continued.

To add a little extra dynamic, we had been allocated an arena where they had been practising jumps, so our session had the added element of dodging jump poles.

What happened next was a game changer. With clear instruction and insight, she broke down each section of the test, told us what the judges were looking for and how to ride it for the maximum marks, then let us each have a go. I found her instruction encouraging and insightful and under her guidance Pudding and I did a half decent dressage test. As our session came to an end I marvelled at the skill of a seasoned instructor, who has heard and seen it all before and knows exactly how to manage people to get the best out of them.

The final walk back to the stables was one on which I took a moment to absorb the last few moments of this experience. The sun was out and wherever you looked there were little hives of activity, it was still quite unbelievable to me that I was actually a part of it. Whilst it had not been the camp I had anticipated, somehow Pudding and I had made it through and learned a lot about ourselves on the way. Just five minutes back in the stable confirmed to me that I was his world, and in many ways, he was mine. I loved that little guy more than words and we had just completed another milestone on our journey together.

The following day things were back to normal and Pudding was delighted to find himself back in his paddock with his field mate, enjoying the newly sprouting spring grass. My phone pinged 'schooling session tonight, can you make it?'

Yes, came the quick reply.

I love this new smaller yard as everyone is so friendly, look out for each other and do so many things together. It is fun to join in and there is nearly always something to join in with. This is the next chapter for Pudding and me, one in which we find ourselves so fortunate to be travelling with another truly lovely set of people, who are becoming very dear friends.

Today it was a quick thirty minutes in the ménage, I had no idea what we were doing but I didn't care, it was always good.

There were only two of us riding tonight and one of the experienced liveries on the ground providing direction. As I entered I saw a jump in the centre of the ménage and a great big smile on my friend's face

"We knew you were disappointed that you didn't get to jump at the camp' she grinned 'so we set one up for you to do tonight"

My heart filled. What amazing ladies, one for being thoughtful enough to set this up and the other to attempt it, as I know she hates jumping.

So what have I learned from the camp? Well, no matter how good you are, there is always more to learn and acres of things you can improve on. Riding horses is a constant process of learning. And the most important lesson – good friends. They pick you up when you are down, encourage you to keep going, share your laughter when the funny things happen, share your exhilaration when you succeed and provide you with a safe place enjoy your horse. It is the people around you that help make the whole experience so completely wonderful.

I got home that evening, full of gratitude and happiness when my phone pinged with a message

'What's all this Princess Caroline of Monaco shit I'm hearing about?'

Chapter Sixteen

Reflections

As I am nearing the eighteen months point with Pudding, I can honestly say they have been life changing. This horse has got under my skin and I absolutely adore him; I adore being with him just grooming him (when you have a grey it is something you do A LOT), I adore being out riding especially on those days when we are really working as one. I adore the fact that I have come to understand him and can sense where he is at – even when there are times when I know we are heading for trouble. It has challenged me in every way, the amount of physical exertion required for constant trips with a loaded wheelbarrow to the muck heap and back has made me so much fitter and that is before you throw in the tone up constant riding gives you. Then there are the mental challenges, getting back in the saddle when your last ride did not go well, or you have had a wobbly moment and lose your confidence. It all adds to the rich tapestry of life and I do feel that any life worth living should not always be about playing it safe but embracing the things you truly want to do. Giving yourself permission to push the boundaries and see what's out there. It is exciting, terrifying and frees your soul.

A few weeks ago, I found myself out with the usual group and one extra, an older lady in her mid-sixties who had only begun riding three years earlier. I was in awe of her, she looked so small and fragile perched on her cob, yet here she was hacking out with us. As we all assembled on the path it just naturally fell that I was closest to the exit and I found myself leading the little party through a busy country park. Our older companion was initially quite nervous, so far she had done most of her riding in the ménage, yet she put her trust in us to look after her today. What happened next surprised me, we encountered dogs running and barking at the horses, bulls running next to the fence only a couple of metres from where we were walking, joggers and cyclists who seemed to creep up behind you and the general noise and bustle of a park full of families enjoying themselves. All of these things would normally register on my radar, but I was so concerned about our companion that looking after her and keeping things calm, that I just didn't notice them. And we all breezed through, without even the slightest moment of worry. I had heard this before, when you are busy looking after someone else, you forget to worry about yourself. But it did make me think about the journey I had been on, that I was nearly two years down the road with Pudding and actually had some idea of how to help someone else – I deployed all the techniques that Janet and Ruth had taught me.

So as this chapter ends it is a good time to reflect on the things that I have learned and hope that should you decide to embark on horse ownership, that some of the learns I have made may prove useful to you.

When viewing a horse, have an expert with you

I learned the hard way that people who want to sell their horse will tell you what you want to hear. I got to the stage where I would refuse to tell people what I wanted the horse for, as I picked up on the fact that whatever you said, that was magically what this horse was 'good' at. But you wouldn't need to be a rocket scientist to figure out that the middle aged woman here to view the horse you described as 'bombproof' and 'anyone's ride' wants a safe, sensible horse. I would strongly advise that you take someone with you who knows what to look for and can help you realistically decide whether that particular horse is suited to you.

Horses are strong and sometime dangerous animals. I know one lady who bought a 'bombproof' horse and ended up with broken ribs and her confidence knocked to bits. Additionally, you do not want to buy one that is going to cost you a fortune in vet bills. In every way possible, it really will save you a lot of heartache if you have someone who knows horses with you and they have permission to tell you the truth.

Buy the horse for where you are now and not where you want to be.

Even the most placid cob can step up a gear if required, but a highly-strung thoroughbred is less likely to be accommodating while you get your act together. There are only so many times you can scare yourself to death before you simply decide to give up.

It is worth really exploring exactly what the horse has done historically before you even view it. Ask for video footage, especially of it doing the thing you are most interested in. So, if that is hacking, then you need to see this horse hack past lorries, tractors, cows etc. and not just a dainty little trot down a deserted country lane.

I laughed recently when a video popped up on Facebook of a young girl who had been refused a horse by her farmer parents, so she had learnt to ride a cow instead. This dairy cow could actually jump higher than I do on Pudding! It seems that with the right application, your beastie will get you well on your way – if not all the way, to your desired destination.

Go at your own pace and if you ever feel too frightened to ride, then don't. Wait for another day and get someone to support you.

With help from others, you can do it. It may even be worth paying an instructor to be present the first time to ride or hack out on your own. It will give you the confidence and guidance you need, until you get to grips with your nerves and how your horse is going to react to things.

I have always preferred to ride with others, it is great to enjoy a ride together but more importantly, if you do get into trouble, there are others who can support you.

There are many times when I have stood in the stable next to my saddled horse and really wanted to dip out of riding. I have had to force myself to do it and usually feel fine after a few minutes in the saddle.

But there have been the odd times when I have decided to give it a couple of days. When Pudding first went out 24/7 for summer grazing, he was really on edge with the increased sugar from the grass and the fact that he probably did not get much sleep for the first couple of nights. He was super spooky, so I left it a couple of days for him to settle.

Pick your livery yard carefully, you will be spending more time there than you can imagine possible right now.

Ideally, you want people who do the things you are interested in, so you have support. Having Ruth and Janet made all the difference to my experience and I am eternally grateful for their friendship and support.

By having a large yard, there are usually people you can ride out with and lots of experience to tap into. I have a bevy of experienced and knowledgeable people to quiz when I need to understand something.

Another thing to consider are the facilities themselves. What is the grazing like and will you feel comfortable going into a field with lots of horses to retrieve yours, or would you prefer to have your horse on its own? I have known people who want to have their horse on its own grazing; they avoid any injury from other horses kicking or biting them.

Personally, I am happy for Pudding to be in with others, but no more than four in a field. Horses are herd animals and they enjoy the company of other horses for mutual grooming and protection. But I have had to deal with my horse being kicked and an owner who has had their horse kicked by mine.

If your little equine friend is having a meltdown when you are on-board, then diffuse the situation by loosening your reins and controlling your breathing.

I have found that slightly looser reins and long, deep breathing are the key to avoiding an escalating drama when you are sat on the horse. Obviously, you don't want them that loose that you have no control, but generally, horses expect to be 'doing something' when you gather the reins up.

If you are leading them, then look forward, keep your shoulders down and breathe long steady breaths.

I am consistently surprised how effective this is.

Your unconscious mind can be developed to help you get where you want to be.

There is an old saying 'if you think you can or you think you can't, you are absolutely right'. So many of the battles we face begin in the mind, so using techniques which help us trick the mind, so we can get to the place where we want to be can be really useful.

One technique is to play through a desired outcome repeatedly until it is embedded deep in your psyche, this will enable you to get on with things and over obstacles. To quote the unconscious mind * "It is always working on behalf of you, processing everything behind the scenes and is always working for your best intentions based upon what it has been directed to do at some point in your life."

Kelly Marks wrote a very interesting piece on this and showed how she used NLP (Neuro Linguistic Practices) to overcome difficulties she had faced and to help her achieve a winning mind-set when she was a jockey. There are lots of NLP books on the market and some great free clips on YouTube if you want to explore this in a little more depth.

I do have moments when things bother me greatly, but I have found using NLP techniques have helped me overcome some of the biggest hurdles and got me moving forward again.

*The NLP Practitioner by Toby & Kate McCartney

Don't worry if the thought of spooking, jumping or giddiness in your horse frightens you to death. It did for me for quite a time, but you will be surprised that a day will dawn when it simply doesn't bother you anymore.

Historically, I have quite literally got off a horse when they showed even the slightest signs of being giddy or spooky.

But stick with it, after a while you get better at your position in the saddle and can cope with it.

You will get there. As my friend once told me, the only way to really learn to ride is to put in the time, *in the saddle.*

Handling horses and collecting your horse from a field full of horses is daunting, but essential to do.

Like riding, the more you do it, the better you will become at it. I look back on my early days and wonder what the hell I was doing. I would stare at other horses and even try to snap my lead rope at them if they came near. I was literally inviting them to take me on! I now ignore them, possibly give them a stroke if they trot up, but carry on and ignore any further attentions.

When horses are crowded around a gate and you need to get yours out, my technique is to get yours closest to the gate and open it, so you can get your horse through and block the others from exiting. I have only had one escapee – and he was a very determined chap!

I would also strongly encourage you not to take food into a field. Horses are powerful animals and food will attract the wrong kind of response. You really do not want to be surrounded by a field full of horses all fighting to get food from you, it is frightening and dangerous.

If food is the only option, then keep the treat behind the gate and give it to your horse when you have got him out of the field and the gate is firmly shut.

And finally, the best for last.

Life really is too short to miss the chance to do something you have always wanted to do. Whilst it has been truly scary at times, I would not have changed it for the world. I am having the time of my life and if you pick the horse for where you are at right now, then so will you.

Don't over think it.

Wishing you mountains of fun

Caroline x

facebook Midlife Crisis Horse

Printed in Great Britain
by Amazon